D0788542

THE
RAILWAY
POCKET BIBLE

THE
POCKET BIBLE
SERIES

THE
RAILWAY
POCKET BIBLE

ANDREW FOWLER

This edition first published in Great Britain 2011 by
Crimson Publishing, a division of Crimson Business Ltd
Westminster House
Kew Road
Richmond
Surrey
TW9 2ND

© Crimson Publishing, 2011

The right of Andrew Fowler to be identified as the author of this work has been asserted by him in accordance with the Copyright, Designs and Patents Act, 1988.

All rights reserved. No part of this publication may be reproduced, transmitted in any form or by any means, or stored in a retrieval system without either the prior written permission of the publisher, or in the case of reprographic reproduction a licence issued in accordance with the terms and licences issued by the CLA Ltd.

A catalogue record for this book is available from the British Library.

ISBN 978 1 907087 233

Typeset by IDSUK (DataConnection) Ltd
Printed and bound by Lego Print SpA, Trento

CONTENTS

INTRODUCTION

Railways have held a fascination since their very earliest days; as a mover of goods and people on a large scale, everything about them inspires a feeling of awe. *The Railway Pocket Bible* explores the amazing world of railways and outlines the major milestones in railway development, which, contrary to popular belief, started long before Stephenson's *Rocket*.

Full of fascinating facts, details and trivia, this book introduces you to the world of railways, including:

- profiles of locomotives, rolling stock and diesel trains;

- the achievements of major engineers such as Brunel and Stephenson;

- an insight into the many and varied roles fulfilled by staff, such as the station master, the driver and the guard;

- the depiction of railways in literature, film and television from *Harry Potter* to *The Railway Children*;

- railway hobbies (no anorak required!), such as photography and 'bashing';

- an introduction to the world of model railways;

- famous trains of old – the routes they took, and how to enjoy the same experience today;

- the speed and glamour of the streamlined trains of the 1930s;

- information on how you can be a steam train driver, whether for a day or regularly.

This book is a must for anyone with an interest in railways, whether you are an experienced enthusiast or making your first foray into this world of excitement and nostalgia.

HISTORY OF THE RAILWAYS

You may already know a lot about today's railways, and you've no doubt heard of George and Robert Stephenson and the famous locomotive *Rocket*, but do you know how the railways have evolved over the past two centuries? This chapter will be your guide through the fascinating history of railways.

⊞⊞⊞ THE EARLIEST YEARS ⊞⊞⊞

Railways have existed in some shape or form for around 2,000 years, although the earliest ones were a far cry from what we know today. The Romans are known to have used slotted paving stones to provide a smooth guided path for horse-drawn wagons, but the idea wasn't developed much further until the middle of the 16th century when rough wooden 'wagonways' began appearing in Germany.

It is Britain, however, that will forever be remembered as the home of the railways. From 1604, a gentleman with the intriguing name of Huntingdon Beaumont introduced wagonways at many coal mines from Nottingham to Tyneside. These bore many similarities to the current systems despite the 'rails' being made of wood: the tracks were laid on a bed of well-drained gravel or 'ballast' and the 'rails' were held at the correct distance by sleepers. The wagons themselves had flanged wheels (see p.169) to stop them derailing; a system that is still used today.

The first railway to use iron rails, designed by an engineer called William Jessop, was introduced in Loughborough in 1789. Jessop was quick to develop his idea further, and as others realised its potential a number of public railway systems were constructed to enable the movement of a variety of goods. Horses were invariably used to haul the wagons on more level lines, with stationary steam engines introduced from the 1770s onwards to haul wagons up steeper inclines.

Pocket Fact 🚂

While steam engines had been around since the end of the 17th century and the first steam vehicle appeared in 1769, it was not until 1804 that the first steam locomotive took to the rails at Pen-y-Darren ironworks in Wales. Its inventor was a Cornishman by the name of Richard Trevithick, and the engine was used to haul a train carrying 10 tons of iron and 70 men a distance of almost 10 miles at a fast walking pace. Frequent stops had to be made due to the heavy locomotive fracturing the brittle iron rails, but the steam locomotive was here to stay.

⊞⊞⊞ THE FIRST LINES ARRIVE ⊞⊞⊞

The first public railway was the 9-mile Surrey Iron Railway, created to carry goods between Wandsworth and Croydon. The line opened in 1803 and had a gauge (the distance between the rails) of 4 feet 2 inches (1,270mm) (see p.4 for more on gauges). The railway didn't have any of its own wagons or even horses to haul them, those wishing to use the line having to supply their own and pay a toll to use the track.

Pocket Fact 🚂

The Swansea & Mumbles Railway is officially the world's first passenger railway; again horses were originally used to pull the trains on this line.

⊞⊞⊞ WHAT GEORGE ⊞⊞⊞ STEPHENSON DID

While the Middleton Railway in Leeds is recognised as being the first railway to use locomotives to haul a small number of its revenue-earning trains as early as 1812, horses were still the principal source of haulage around the world. The next big developments in the world of railways were down to a man named George Stephenson. Forever remembered as the builder of the famous steam engine *Rocket*, Stephenson was nonetheless responsible for far more than that; in fact he is often described as the 'Father of the Railways'.

In 1814, George Stephenson built his first steam engine to work at a Tyneside colliery. Named the *Blücher*, it could haul 30 tons of coal every trip and was so successful that 16 further examples were built by 1820. In 1822, Stephenson made history when his railway between Sunderland and Hetton opened, as it was the first railway not to use horses to haul some of its trains. However, gravity was used to move some trains downhill so it wasn't the first line to use solely locomotive power for freight trains; that honour was to go to the Stockton & Darlington Railway.

THE STOCKTON & DARLINGTON RAILWAY

George Stephenson surveyed the route of the 25-mile Stockton & Darlington Railway in 1821 and the line opened on 27 September 1825. The original intention was for horses to haul all of the trains, but Stephenson's influence led to the decision to use steam locomotives as the sole motive power. The first and most famous of these was *Locomotion No 1*, built at the works of Stephenson's son, Robert. The line was built with the intention of carrying freight, though a passenger carriage was constructed at the outset and used to convey dignitaries at the opening. Horses were used initially to haul passenger trains and the gauge used was standard gauge (see below).

Stephenson's standard gauge

The term 'gauge' refers to the distance between the rails on each track. George Stephenson's chosen gauge was originally 4 feet 8 inches (1,422mm), as this was how far apart the wheels of the early 'chaldron' wagons in the Tyneside mines were. Following problems on the Stockton & Darlington line where the wheel flanges could drag on tight curves, the rails but not the wheels were moved another half inch (13mm) further apart to make the now-familiar standard gauge of 4 feet 8½ inches (1,435mm).

ⰟⰟⰟⰟ TIMELINE OF PRINCIPAL ⰟⰟⰟⰟ RAILWAY DEVELOPMENTS AFTER 1825

3 May 1830: Canterbury & Whitstable Railway opens.

A 5¾-mile line designed by George Stephenson, the Canterbury & Whitstable Railway, uses stationary engines to cable-haul wagons up inclines with a small 4-wheeled locomotive moving some trains along short level sections of track.

15 September 1830: Liverpool & Manchester Railway opens.

The opening of the Liverpool & Manchester Railway was the world's first inter-city passenger railway. Engineered by George Stephenson with assistance from his son Robert, it contained some major engineering features including a floating embankment across Chat Moss bog (still in use today) and a 2,250-yard (2,057m) tunnel at Wapping. It was also the first line to use steam locomotives throughout, though as the railway board were not convinced about their suitability the Rainhill Trials were organised (see box below). The railway was very successful, and ensured the rapid development of lines throughout the world.

The Rainhill Trials

In order to assess the reliability and performance of the steam locomotives of the time, the sceptical board of the Liverpool & Manchester Railway organised a trial in 1829, the year before the line opened. It took place on a 1¾-mile long section of the nearly complete line at Rainhill near Liverpool. Out of 10 locomotives originally entered in the competition, only five actually took part:

1. *George and Robert Stephenson's* Rocket
2. *Timothy Hackworth's* Sans Pareil
3. *Timothy Burstall's* Perseverance
4. *John Ericsson and John Braithwaite's* Novelty
5. *Thomas Shaw Brandreth's* Cycloped

The last of these, Cycloped, *was intriguing as it wasn't a steam locomotive at all; it actually used a horse on a treadmill to turn the wheels. Unsurprisingly, it was unable to keep pace with the steam-powered entrants and was declared unsuitable.* Rocket *was the outright winner as it was the only one to complete the whole series of tests without breaking down.* Rocket's *designers won £500 and the contract to supply locomotives to the line.*

1830: The first railroads appear in America, including the Baltimore & Ohio.

1834: The first railway in Germany, the Bavarian Ludwigsbahn, opens.

1834: Railways appear in Ireland with the advent of the Dublin & Kingstown Railway. Built to standard gauge, it is relaid to Irish Gauge in 1854.

Pocket Fact 📖

In Ireland, the 5 feet 3 inches (1,600mm) 'Irish Gauge' is widely employed. It's also used on some lines in Brazil and Australia.

1836: The first railway in London opens, running from Spa Road to Deptford (later part of the London & Greenwich Railway). The London & Greenwich Railway is the first elevated railway in the world, with 3¾ miles of line being laid on an 878-arch brick viaduct.

1837: The Grand Junction Railway opens between Birmingham and Warrington. This is the first section of what becomes the main London–Birmingham–Liverpool and Manchester main line.

4 June 1838: The first section of the famous Great Western Railway opens from London Paddington to Maidenhead with Isambard Kingdom Brunel (see p.83) as engineer. The track is laid to Brunel's famous broad gauge.

Broad gauge

Isambard Kingdom Brunel favoured what became known as broad gauge. At 7 feet 0¼ inches (2,140mm), Brunel used this gauge when building railways, believing it could give trains a better level of comfort and stability at speed. Much of the early Great Western Railway was laid like this, together with a small number of other lines such as the Bristol & Gloucester Railway.

Initially, the gauge differences didn't matter as most lines were constructed individually and were separate from each other. Problems arose when the Bristol & Gloucester Railway met with the standard gauge Birmingham & Gloucester Railway; passengers were forced to change trains to continue their journeys in either direction. This was unpopular and marked the start of the 'Gauge War', with supporters of both gauges arguing their merits. While some track was laid to mixed gauge (able to carry both broad and standard gauge trains) as a temporary solution, as the vast majority of lines in the UK were already built to Stephenson's standard gauge the decision was made to adopt this as the British standard. All broad and mixed gauge track was subsequently dismantled, but some replica track has recently been installed at Didcot Railway Centre. The Great Western was forced to re-gauge all its track and Brunel's broad gauge disappeared on 20 May 1892.

1839: The first telegraph system is brought into use on the Great Western Railway, paving the way for modern signalling.

1841: Brunel's Disc and Crossbar signal (see p.31), the first to give a positive clear indication, is introduced on the Great Western Railway.

1841: The first semaphore signal (see pp32–33) is introduced at New Cross in South London by the London & Croydon Railway.

1842: Queen Victoria becomes the first British monarch to travel by train.

1846: 'Railway Mania' reaches its zenith, with a huge number of lines proposed and constructed – in this year 272 lines totalling over 9,500 route miles were passed by Act of Parliament.

1848: The Caledonian Railway opens its Carlisle–Glasgow and Edinburgh lines, completing the main West Coast London to Scotland route.

1850: The East Coast railway from London to Edinburgh opens.

1854: The first railways open in Australia.

1857: Steel rails begin to replace wrought iron ones in Britain, allowing heavier trains to run.

1863: The Metropolitan Railway becomes the first underground railway in Britain. The trains are steam-hauled and the smoke causes problems in the long tunnels (see p.71).

1866: The narrow gauge Talyllyn Railway opens in Wales, becoming the first such line in Britain to be authorised to operate steam-hauled passenger trains.

Narrow gauge

Other than the standard gauge implemented by George Stephenson (see p.4), there have been a number of other gauges used over the years. Anything less than standard gauge is usually referred to as 'narrow' gauge; this starts as small as 15 inches (381mm), the gauge used by a number of miniature railways such as the Romney, Hythe and Dymchurch and Ravenglass and Eskdale railways.

There were many quarry railways in the British Isles using a gauge of 1 foot 11½ inches (597mm), 2 feet (610mm), 2 feet 3 inches (686mm) and 2 feet 6 inches (762mm), some of which are now in use as tourist passenger railways, particularly in Wales. Notable among these is the Welsh Highland Railway, currently the longest preserved railway in Britain at 40 miles. Metre gauge (3 feet 3⅜ inches or 1,000mm) is employed extensively in Europe while 3 foot gauge (914mm) is used on the Isle of Man and has also seen use elsewhere, including America and Spain.

1868: The first section of the New York elevated railway is opened. Trains are initially cable-hauled, with steam locomotives taking over from 1870.

1869: The first Transcontinental Railroad opens in America, running from Omaha in Nebraska to Sacramento in California.

1869: The first of Queen Victoria's Royal Trains is constructed by the London & North Western Railway.

1874: The first bogie coaches (see p.167) are introduced by the Midland Railway.

1879: The first Tay Bridge collapses in a high wind; a train is crossing at the time and all 75 people on board are killed.

1883: Magnus Volk opens his 'Electric Railway' in Brighton; the 2-mile line is officially the world's first electric tramway and is still operating today.

1885: The first section of the Blackpool Tramway opens, making it the first electric street tramway in the world.

1888: The first 'Race to the North', between daytime London–Aberdeen trains, takes place.

1890: The City & South London Railway (now part of London Underground's Northern Line) opens, becoming both the first 'Tube' railway and the first underground electric railway in the world.

1891: Work starts on the Trans-Siberian Railway in Russia. Construction of the 5,787-mile (9,313km) route takes 10 years to complete.

1892: The Chicago 'L' elevated railway opens in America.

1893: The Liverpool Overhead Railway opens, the only elevated railway in Britain and the first railway in the world to use electric multiple units (see p.40).

1895: The second 'Race to the North', between overnight London–Aberdeen trains on the west and east coast routes, takes place.

1899: The Great Central Railway's Marylebone station becomes the last main line terminus to be built in London, as part of the joint railway constructed with the Great Western (now the Chiltern line).

1901: The first steam railmotors (see p.170) enter service on the London & South Western Railway. Despite many railways subsequently adopting them they were ultimately unsuccessful and most were withdrawn after less than 10 years' service.

1901: Queen Victoria dies and her casket is transported from Paddington by the Royal Train.

1904: The first electric suburban railway is opened on Tyneside by the North Eastern Railway. A third rail system (see pp26–27) is chosen.

Pocket Fact

On 9 May 1904, the Great Western Railway locomotive No 3440 City of Truro *became the first to break the 100mph barrier, attaining a maximum speed of 102.3mph on the 'Ocean Mails' special train between Plymouth and Paddington. The speed was unofficially recorded by timing the train over a distance and, while sometimes disputed, is generally accepted as correct.*

1906: The Great Western Railway trials Automatic Train Control on the Henley branch.

1907: The Great Western Railway introduces the 'Star' class 4-6-0 (see p.46), the first of its highly successful express passenger locomotives of similar appearance. The design evolves into the 'Castle' class in 1923.

1908: The Great Western Railway introduces the first 'Pacific' type locomotive (see p.46) in Britain. Called *The Great Bear* it is ultimately unsuccessful and is not repeated on the GWR but this wheel arrangement is used with great success by other companies.

1908: The Midland Railway electrifies its Lancaster–Morecambe and Heysham lines using a catenary system (see pp29–30), rated at 6,600 volts AC.

1914: With the outbreak of the First World War, Britain's railways come under government control.

1914: The first electric services run on the London & North Western Railway between Willesden and Earl's Court.

1915: The first of the London & South Western Railway's electric services commence. These use a third rail system (see pp26–27), and from these the current system of electrified lines in southern England spread.

1915: Britain's worst ever rail disaster occurs at Quintishill, Scotland. Five trains were involved and 226 people were killed.

1918: The First World War ends. During the war a shortage of staff and raw materials meant that maintenance was lacking and the railways were worn out. Government control continues until 1921.

1921: The Railways Act 1921 is passed. Nationalisation is rejected in favour of what becomes known as the 'Grouping', where four companies would run all the railways in Britain (with a few exceptions).

The 1923 Grouping

The Grouping saw over 120 individual railway companies become just four on 1 January 1923. The new companies, dubbed the 'Big Four', were the London, Midland & Scottish Railway (LMS), London & North Eastern Railway (LNER), Southern Railway (SR) and Great Western Railway (GWR). The latter was the only company to keep its identity under the 1921 Railways Act.

The LMS was the largest of the four with over 7,700 miles of track, and was in charge of the West Coast Main Line from London Euston to Glasgow, together with the former Midland Main Line from London St Pancras to Derby, Sheffield and Carlisle and numerous smaller lines into Wales and Scotland. The LNER was the next largest company with over 6,500 miles of track. It looked after the East Coast Main Line between London King's Cross and Edinburgh as well as lines into East Anglia, north to Aberdeen and in fact most lines east of the Pennines. The Great Western changed the least, having absorbed a large number of its competitors previously, but inherited a number of routes in Wales, including the scenic Cambrian Railway and other, mainly freight-carrying, lines into the Welsh coalfields. The Southern Railway was the smallest of the four companies with just under 2,200 route miles of line. As its name suggested, it looked after all the lines south of London that weren't owned by the GWR; while its principal routes were from London Victoria and Waterloo to the ports of Dover, Portsmouth and Southampton it also operated into Devon and Cornwall.

Some joint railways remained independent, including the famous Somerset and Dorset Railway, which continued to be operated jointly by the LMS and Southern Railways.

1923: The famous Pacific locomotive (see p.46) *Flying Scotsman* enters service on the LNER (see box above). Unnamed at first, it carries the number 1472.

1926: The LMS introduces its 'all steel carriage', representing a significant improvement on previous British designs.

1927: The Great Western Railway introduces the last and largest of its express passenger designs, the 4-6-0 'King' class (see p.46).

1928: The inaugural non-stop 'Flying Scotsman' service runs between London King's Cross and Edinburgh hauled by the famous locomotive of the same name (see p.51). To facilitate the non-stop run, No 4472 *Flying Scotsman* is fitted with a special corridor tender.

Pocket Fact 🎀

To enable non-stop running of its prestige services, the LNER introduced corridor tenders (see p.168) from 1928. These carried nine tons of coal, a ton more than the largest previously used, and included a cramped corridor running down the right-hand side of the tender, 5 feet (1.52m) high and 18 inches (460mm) wide to allow a locomotive crew to change while on the move on long journeys. The relief crew travelled in the front coach of the train, swapping halfway through the journey with those on the footplate (see p.169).

1929: Two of the 'Big Four' experiment with ultra-high pressure steam locomotives; the LMS producing a 4-6-0, No 6399 *Fury* and the LNER with the unnamed W1 No 10000 (nicknamed 'Hush Hush' because of the secrecy surrounding its construction) (see p.47). Both were rebuilt as standard locomotives by 1936.

1931: The LMS introduces its first diesel shunting locomotive. Rebuilt from a withdrawn steam locomotive, it is in itself unsuccessful but leads to other designs, including the standard LMS shunter of 1945 which itself is the forerunner of the present Class 08.

1933: The LMS introduce a small number of 4-wheeled diesel railcars (see p.169) for use on rural services, initially operating on the Blackburn to Clitheroe line in north-west England.

1933: The Southern Railway introduces the first electric main line service between London and Brighton.

1934: The LNER's *Flying Scotsman* becomes the first locomotive to officially reach the 100mph mark, 30 years after *City of Truro*'s unofficial record.

1934: The Great Western Railway introduces the first successful diesel railcars for express branch line services. Their streamlined appearance and chocolate and cream livery leads to their nickname of 'Flying Bananas'.

1935: Sir Nigel Gresley, Chief Mechanical Engineer of the LNER, introduces the first of his famous streamlined 'A4' class locomotives. The first four are painted silver to work the 'Silver Jubilee' prestige train (see p.102).

Pocket Fact 🎗

In 1935, Sir William Stanier (see p.85) introduced a modified 'Princess' class locomotive, No 6202, which used turbines instead of cylinders to provide drive to the wheels. Unlike earlier experiments, the Turbomotive was a great success, and covered over 300,000 miles between 1935 and 1949. In that year, one of the turbines broke and, with Stanier no longer in charge by that time, it was decided to rebuild it as a conventional locomotive. Re-entering service in 1952 as 46202 Princess Anne, *it was wrecked just two months later in the Harrow rail disaster.*

1935: One of Gresley's 'A4' locomotives, 2509 *Silver Link* breaks the speed record by achieving 112.5mph on a press run to publicise the new 'Silver Jubilee' service, starting a renewed 'Race to the North'.

1937: The LMS break the LNER's speed record, with Sir William Stanier's 'Princess Coronation' class No 6220 *Coronation* on a press run of the new 'Coronation Scot' prestige train achieving a maximum speed of 114mph.

1938: Gresley's 'A4' locomotive 4468 *Mallard* sets an all-time world speed record for steam traction, achieving 126mph during high-speed braking trials. The consistently fast performance of this streamlined class of locomotives leads to their being nicknamed 'Streaks'.

1938: Automatic Train Control is adopted on all GWR main lines (see p.167).

1939: With the outbreak of the Second World War, the railways come once more under government control. Prestige trains cease to run, with many of the coaches put in storage, never to run again. During the war, many LMS locomotives lose their streamlining to ease maintenance.

1941: The LNER's first new main line electric locomotive, EM1 No 6701, is completed. Designed with the future electrification of the Manchester–Sheffield and Wath electrification scheme (see p.68) in mind it is initially tested on the Manchester–Altrincham line and then stored until after the war.

1941: The first of Oliver Bulleid's 'Merchant Navy' class locomotives (see p.58) enter service despite austerity conditions. The unusual appearance of the locomotives leads to their nickname 'Spamcans'.

1941: Alongside the new steam locomotives, the first of a class of new electric locomotive design enters traffic on the Southern Railway. Numbered CC1, it is needed to cope with the unusual freight demand caused by wartime conditions on the only one of the 'Big Four' railways that carries more passengers than goods.

1942: Bulleid follows the success of his 'Merchant Navy' locomotive with the last development of the British 0-6-0, the highly-unusual 'Q1' class. Despite their unusual appearance, which leads to their nickname of 'Coffee Pots', they prove very powerful and highly successful.

1943: Robert Riddles, working at the Ministry of Supply, is responsible for the design of his first locomotives, the 'Austerity' 2-8-0s and 2-10-0s (see p.46), which subsequently number over 1,100 examples.

Pocket Fact

During the Second World War, materials were in short supply and factories were busy supplying munitions, tanks, ships and aircraft for the war effort. Nonetheless, locomotives were needed too, to transport troops and munitions both in Britain and Europe. Robert Riddles designed the rugged 'Austerity' 2-8-0 and 2-10-0 locomotives for hauling heavy trains, many hundreds of which were shipped abroad after D-Day. For less arduous purposes, the Hunslet company of Leeds produced 0-6-0 saddle tanks (see pp38 and 46). All were designed to be cheap and quick to manufacture using the limited materials available with a short service life assumed, but many survived into the 1960s and beyond.

1945: With the end of the Second World War, the 'Big Four' companies resume control of the railways.

1947: The first main line diesel locomotive, No 10000, enters service on the LMS railway. An identical locomotive, No 10001, is completed the following year.

1948: Following on from the Transport Act 1947, the 'Big Four' railways, together with the remaining joint lines, are nationalised to form one government-owned company, British Railways. The name changes to British Rail in the 1960s.

1949: The first gas turbine locomotive enters service on British Railways. Ordered by the GWR in 1946, its production was delayed by a shortage of materials following the war. Numbered 18000, it is unreliable in service and is withdrawn in 1960. It is unnamed but given the nickname 'Kerosene Castle' by spotters. Another example, 18100, entered traffic in 1951.

1950: The first Southern Region diesel locomotives are introduced. Due to the weight of the available diesel engines and electric generators, motors and control equipment, they adopt a 1Co–Co1 wheel arrangement (see p.63). The design is later developed to produce the English Electric Type 4 (later Class 40) locomotive.

1951: The narrow gauge (see p.8) Talyllyn Railway in Wales is the first railway in the world to be preserved.

Railway preservation

The Talyllyn Railway was a privately-owned narrow gauge line and was taken on by a group of dedicated individuals with the aim of keeping it running after closure by its original owners. The desire was not to modernise it but to keep it going in the same way it had been run over the years – in other words, preserved for posterity and for the benefit of all. It was early days, but a significant amount of the national network would soon follow suit.

As the 1960s dawned, the closure of branch lines accelerated. Many of them, though unprofitable for British Railways, were the lifeblood of the communities they served and their loss was felt significantly. With the closure of the lines came widespread scrapping of steam locomotives and rolling stock, and preservation groups began to spring up all round the country, with the aim of saving trains, railways and artefacts. Most were entirely non-profit making and run by volunteers, and remain so to this day.

1952: The first section of main line to be electrified by British Railways, between Penistone and Wath, is energised. This is the first part of the Manchester–Sheffield and Wath line to use electric traction.

1952: The worst railway disaster in England takes place at Harrow and Wealdstone station, 11 miles outside London on the West Coast Main Line (London Euston to Glasgow Central via Crewe and Preston). The accident was caused by a driver failing to stop at a danger signal in thick fog.

1953: The first English Electric 350hp diesel shunting (later Class 08) locomotives enter service. The class eventually numbers 996 examples, many of which are still in use today.

1954: The Woodhead Route is electrified. The Manchester–Sheffield and Wath line (the Woodhead Route) opens throughout as 'Britain's first all-electric main line', electrified at 1500V DC (see p.69). A new 3-mile long double-track tunnel is bored at Woodhead as the old twin bores are unsuitable for carrying the overhead catenary (see pp29–30). A fleet of new mixed traffic locomotives to a similar design to the LNER prototype 6701, and seven larger passenger locomotives, are used to haul the trains.

1954: The last steam express passenger locomotive to be built by British Railways, the unique Riddles 'Pacific' 71000 *Duke of Gloucester*, enters traffic.

1954: British Railways introduces its first diesel multiple units (see p.168).

1954: The 1955 Modernisation Plan is published in December. The plan advocates widespread electrification of routes and the introduction of diesel locomotives and multiple units to speed up services, together with the abolition of steam traction.

1955: English Electric unveils the prototype 'Deltic' diesel; at the time of its launch it is the most powerful single unit diesel locomotive in the world, with two engines developing a total of 3,300hp. Its striking blue and silver livery draws a lot of attention as it goes on trial on the West Coast Main Line.

1956: The Liverpool Overhead Railway, the only line of its type in Britain, closes following the discovery that complete renewal of the structure's deck is required at a cost of £2 million.

1957: A train crash at Lewisham kills 90 people when a driver misses signals in fog and collides with another train, bringing down a bridge over the line in the process. The subsequent inquiry speeds up the introduction of the Automatic Warning System (see p.167).

1958: The first of the Modernisation Plan diesel locomotives enter service, the English Electric Type 4s (later Class 40s) D200–209. The design is successful and the class eventually numbers 200 examples.

1958: In preparation for the electrification of the West Coast Main Line between London Euston and Glasgow Central using the new 25kV AC standard (see p.69), the Western Region gas turbine locomotive No 18100 is converted to direct electric propulsion.

1958: The Western Region's first express passenger diesel locomotives, the D600 'Warships' are delivered. The Western Region opts for hydraulic transmission for its locomotives to save weight compared with the diesel electric power trains (see p.39) used by other lines, and the D600s are an unsuccessful experiment. All are withdrawn by 1967, replaced with the D800 'Warships' and the D1000 'Westerns'.

1958–1959: The first sections of the West Coast Main Line, those from Crewe to Liverpool and Manchester, are completed and energised.

1959: The first batch of new electric locomotives, the 25 AL1s (later Class 81s) enter service. With most of the electrification work on the West Coast Main Line outstanding they are trialled and used for driver training on the Crewe–Manchester line.

1960: The last steam locomotive to be built by British Railways, No 92220 *Evening Star* a '9F' heavy freight locomotive designed by Robert Riddles, is outshopped from Swindon works. It holds the distinction of being the only locomotive to be selected for preservation at the time of its construction. It is withdrawn in 1965.

1960: The Bluebell Railway in Sussex becomes the first standard gauge line to be preserved.

Pocket Fact 🏛

In 1953, Ealing Studios released a light-hearted comedy film, The Titfield Thunderbolt, *which featured an early preservation attempt. The story shows a group of villagers purchasing a branch line, locomotive and rolling stock and portrays the struggle to keep it running against opposition from locals and the bus company. While it was inspired by the saving of the*

Talyllyn line it was eerily similar to what would happen on the Bluebell Railway seven years later.

1961–1962: A fleet of 22 100mph-plus D9000 'Deltics' (later Class 55s) is introduced on the East Coast Main Line, following the decision to delay electrification of the route. Their speed and reliability are such that they replace 55 steam locomotives.

1963: The report *The Reshaping of Britain's Railways* (more commonly known as the 'Beeching Report') is published.

The Beeching axe

The Beeching Report showed many lines to be unprofitable and recommended widespread closure of stations, goods yards and lines. While many of these were only branch lines, the railway was often a lifeline into rural areas. Some popular main lines and holiday routes also closed, such as the Somerset and Dorset Railway (see p.96). More than 6,000 miles of line closed between 1963 and 1973. However, as the 1970s began the realisation dawned that road traffic congestion was building to the extent that further closures were undesirable. The closed branches dramatically reduced the 'feeder' traffic onto the remaining lines, and failed to achieve the anticipated cost saving. In recent years several closed lines and stations have been reopened in addition to those that were preserved, including the section of line through Snow Hill Tunnel in London and part of the Argyle Line in Scotland, and a new station has been opened in Birmingham to replace the long-closed Snow Hill.

1963: The famous 'A3' Pacific *Flying Scotsman* is preserved by Alan Pegler, restored to LNER condition and returned to steam. It hauls a number of railtours on the main line beyond the end of steam.

1964: The first Japanese 'Bullet Train' enters service on the Shinkansen (New Main Line).

1965: The Western Region becomes the first area of British Railways to completely oust steam traction from its trains.

1967: Electrification of the section of the West Coast Main Line south of Crewe is completed.

1967: Steam ends on the Southern Region of British Railways.

1968: Steam officially ends on British Railways on 4 August. A special train runs on 11 August known as the 'Fifteen Guinea Special' due to the high price of tickets. The last three steam depots, Rose Grove, Lostock Hall and Carnforth, close.

1970: Passenger traffic ceases on the Manchester–Sheffield electrified main line and Sheffield Victoria station is closed.

1972: British Rail builds an experimental tilting train. Powered by gas turbine engines, the APT-E (Advanced Passenger Train – Experimental). Three years later the train attains a speed of 152.3mph on the main line out of London Paddington, a British record at the time.

1973: British Rail introduces the Total Operations Processing System (TOPS), leading to the adoption of locomotive and rolling stock numbering used to the present day.

1974: The electrification of the West Coast Main Line is completed from Weaver Junction to Glasgow Central. A fleet of 26 new Class 87 locomotives is introduced to work the extended route.

1976: The first British Rail 'InterCity 125' High Speed Train enters service. The trains have a power car (effectively a single-ended locomotive) at each end and are capable of a top speed of 143mph, but are restricted to 125mph in normal service. Their introduction on the East Coast Main Line sees the withdrawal of the 'Deltics' in 1980–1981.

1977: The last of the Western Region diesel hydraulic locomotives is withdrawn. Diesel electric transmission is now standardised throughout Britain on non-electrified routes.

1978: The first section of the East Coast Main Line, between King's Cross and Royston, is electrified.

1979: The prototype electric Advanced Passenger Trains (APT-P) enter service on the London Euston–Glasgow Central Main Line, soon setting a British speed record of 162.2mph.

1981: The first French TGV (Train à Grande Vitesse – high speed train) enters service.

1981: The Manchester–Wath line is closed just 27 years after electrification due to the decline in freight traffic. The section from Manchester to Hadfield and Glossop remains open to passengers and is re-energised at 25kV AC.

1983: The Midland Main Line between London St Pancras and Bedford is electrified.

1985–1986: The APT-P trains are deemed unsuccessful following difficulties with the transmission and tilting mechanism and all are withdrawn. The technology is sold to the car and engine manufacturer Fiat for use in their Pendolino trains.

1987: The East Coast Main Line electrification is extended to Peterborough; Newcastle and York are reached two years later.

1987–1990: A fleet of 50 Class 90 electric locomotives is introduced on the West Coast Main Line to replace the original 100 members of classes 81–85 introduced in 1960.

1988: The first 'InterCity 225' trains enter service on the West Coast Main Line. Consisting of a Class 91 locomotive at one end, a rake of coaches and an unpowered driving car at the opposite end, the new trains are capable of 140mph (225km/h).

1991: The East Coast Main Line electrification is completed when the overhead wires reach Edinburgh.

1993: The Railways Act 1993 is passed, allowing the privatisation of British Rail. Initially, the railways are 'sectorised' (split up) to facilitate this in the future.

1994: Privatisation of British Rail begins with ownership of track and structures passing to Railtrack. Train operations are franchised to a number of companies between 1994 and 1997.

1994: The 31.4-mile (50.5km) Channel Tunnel opens, providing a rail link between England and France. A new station is opened in London for passenger trains at Waterloo International, and vehicle terminals are opened at Cheriton (near Folkestone) in England and Coquelles (near Calais) in France.

1999: A Thames train crashes into a First Great Western train at Ladbroke Grove in West London, killing 31 people. The Thames train had gone through a red signal after leaving Paddington station.

2001: The government withdraws funding from Railtrack in the aftermath of the Hatfield rail crash, effectively sending Railtrack into administration.

2002: A London to King's Lynn train operated by WAGN derails near Potters Bar, Hertfordshire, killing 7 people. Faulty points were found to be the cause.

2003: The first 46-mile (74km) section of the High Speed 1 railway line, the Channel Tunnel Rail Link, opens. Trains continue to use the low speed suburban lines through London to access Waterloo International terminus.

2007: The 23-mile (39.4km) second section of the High Speed 1 rail link between the Channel Tunnel and the new terminus of London St Pancras International is completed. It allows speeds of up to 186mph (300km/h) to be reached.

2007: A modified TGV sets a world speed record for an electric train, reaching 357.2mph (574km/h).

2007: Network Rail is fined £4 million for safety breaches that led to the Paddington crash in 1999. The crash highlighted the usefulness of the Train Protection Warning System which would automatically apply the brakes to a train passing a red signal.

2011: Network Rail is fined £3 million for safety failings over the Potters Bar rail crash in 2002.

While these modern accidents can seem frightening, they have all led to more stringent safety procedures, making rail travel safer than ever.

⊞⊞⊞ THE CHANGING PURPOSE ⊞⊞⊞ OF THE RAILWAYS

The earliest railways were constructed to carry freight, such as coal and iron, which were the two most important commodities in the Industrial Revolution. The Stockton & Darlington Railway was conceived mainly as a carrier of goods, though passengers were carried from the outset in small numbers. As reliability and speed of the trains increased, they became the desirable method for transporting more and more goods. They were an early carrier of the mail, speeding up the postal service and reducing the risk of robbery. Before long, trains were transporting vast quantities of perishables, such as milk, meat and fish over long distances in specially-designed wagons.

The Liverpool & Manchester Railway was the first railway built with passengers intended as the principal traffic, but there were surprisingly few others. The Liverpool Overhead Railway, the underground railways in London and the suburban lines around London, Manchester, Glasgow and other regional capitals were among others that carried little or no freight, being intended for passenger use from the outset. This remained true into the early 1950s.

However, after the Second World War, road haulage came to the fore and the railways' freight monopoly gradually ended. Ex-military lorries were snapped up by prospective hauliers and the new road-building programme provided long-distance motorways of a quality previously only dreamed of. When the Beeching axe fell from 1963, thousands of stations, lines and goods yards were swept away and freight services were withdrawn. By the early 1970s British Rail was left with hundreds of almost new diesel locomotives for which there was no longer any use. Some were sold for industrial use but many were scrapped.

Passenger services reached a low in the early 1970s too, but numbers gradually increased with the introduction of the new High Speed Trains at the end of the decade. The network was sectorised in 1982, InterCity, Network SouthEast and Provincial (later called Regional Railways) arrived, and all were popular with passengers. In particular, Network SouthEast swelled passenger numbers.

The situation improved further following significant investment in trains and infrastructure after privatisation. With rising fuel prices and increasing congestion on the roads, freight has returned to the railways in the new millennium to the extent that major routes like the West Coast Main Line are operating at maximum capacity.

⊞⊞⊞ ELECTRIFICATION ⊞⊞⊞

Electrification of railways is seen as a modern way of speeding up and improving services, but even when electricity was in its infancy in the Victorian era it was recognised that electric trains had significant advantages. Electrification of railways began in the last decade of the 19th century; following the arrival of trams many lines were suffering from loss of passengers due to competition.

Top 10 early electrified railways

1. *Volk's Electric Railway, Brighton; 1883*
2. *City & South London Railway (now part of London Underground's Northern Line); 1893*
3. *Liverpool Overhead Railway; 1893*
4. *North Eastern Railway; Tyneside Electrification; 1904*
5. *Midland Railway; Lancaster–Morecambe and Heysham line; 1908*
6. *London, Brighton & South Coast Railway 'Elevated Electrics'; 1909*
7. *Lancashire and Yorkshire Railway; Bury to Holcombe Brook; 1913*
8. *London & South Western Railway; 1915 to present*
9. *North Eastern Railway; Shildon to Newport; 1915*
10. *Lancashire & Yorkshire Railway; Manchester Victoria to Bury; 1917*

While most early systems used relatively low supply voltages and direct current (DC) supply due to the technology available at the time, the three basic methods of electricity supply used on the Victorian and Edwardian lines have remained basically unchanged. These are:

1. **Third rail.** An extra rail is laid alongside the running rails to carry the electric current, and the supply is collected by a 'shoe' on the locomotive or power car rubbing along the top of the rail. The return current is carried by the running rails. This is used extensively on the railways to the south of London.

2. **Fourth rail.** As third rail, but with an extra rail laid between the running rails to carry the return current. This system is used on the London Underground to avoid the risk of return current in the running rails being short-circuited to the cast iron tube tunnel walls.

THIRD RAIL

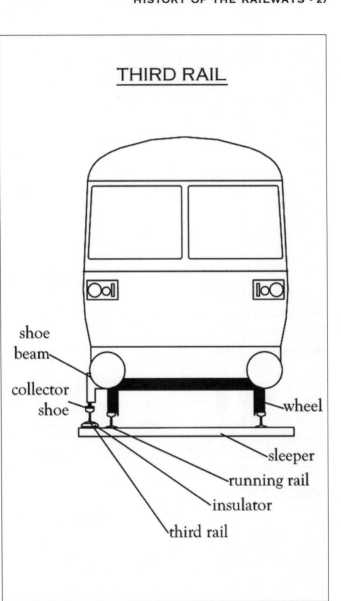

shoe beam

collector shoe

wheel

sleeper

running rail

insulator

third rail

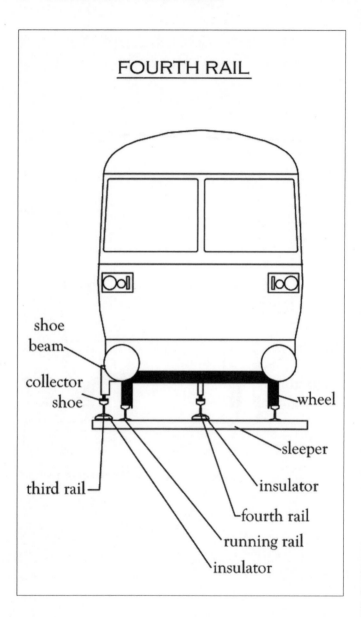

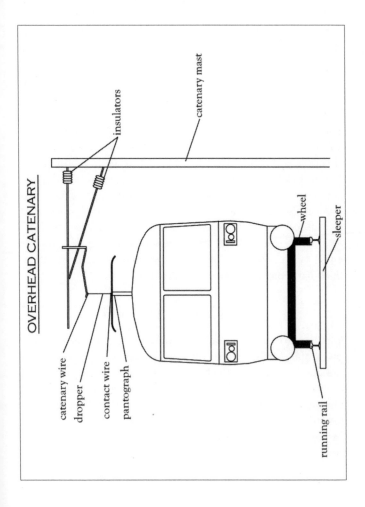

OVERHEAD CATENARY

insulators

catenary mast

catenary wire

dropper

contact wire

pantograph

wheel

sleeper

running rail

3. **Overhead catenary.** The electric current is carried by a contact wire suspended from a series of gantries above the train, which carries a pantograph arm that transfers the supply to the controllers and motors. This system is used on the West and East Coast Main Lines and brand new lines such as High Speed 1.

In the 1930s, it was decided that overhead catenary, energised at 1,500V DC, would be the new national standard. The LNER commenced the electrification of the Manchester, Sheffield and Wath railway (often known as the Woodhead Route after the famous tunnels on the line) in 1936, even producing a prototype locomotive, but the Second World War intervened and the scheme was finally completed by British Railways in 1954. Despite being a modern system at its conception, the flagship scheme was rapidly outdated due to post-war technological advances. Just a year later, the 1955 Modernisation Plan declared the national standard supply for the future would be 25kV AC (Alternating Current) and after only four years the first sections of the West Coast Main Line were energised on the new system, which has remained the standard ever since.

⊞⊞⊞⊞ SIGNALLING ⊞⊞⊞⊞

From the earliest days of railways, where more than one train was run on the same track a method was needed to keep them from running into one another. The first method was the 'Time Interval' system, where a train was allowed to leave a station a set time after the previous one had departed. The obvious flaw with this method was that if a train broke down between stations (extremely common with unreliable early locomotives) collisions could, and did, occur.

Signals were only usually introduced after pressure from legislation. Brunel introduced a 'Disc and Crossbar' signal on his Great Western Railway, but the first successful type was the 'semaphore' signal, which uses a pivoting arm mounted at the top of a tall post. Two types of 'home' (stop) semaphores are used, both of which

BRUNEL'S 'DISC AND CROSSBAR' SIGNALS

Danger (stop)

Line clear

KEY TO COLOURS

☐ White	▨ Green
■ Black	▨ Red
☐ Yellow	

UPPER QUADRANT SEMAPHORES

Distant signals

Caution - prepare to
stop at next signal

Line clear

Home signals

Danger (stop)

Line clear

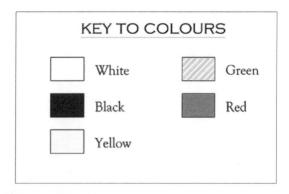

KEY TO COLOURS

White

Green

Black

Red

Yellow

LOWER QUADRANT SEMAPHORES

Distant signals

Caution - prepare to
stop at next signal

Line clear

Home signals

Danger (stop)

Line clear

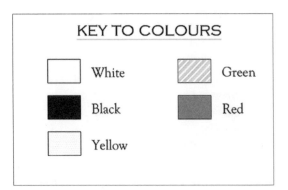

KEY TO COLOURS

White

Green

Black

Red

Yellow

MODERN 4-ASPECT COLOUR LIGHT SIGNALS

Green - line clear for at least the next 3 signals

Double amber - Caution. Prepare to stop 2 signals ahead

Amber - Caution. Prepare to stop at next signal

Red - Danger (stop)

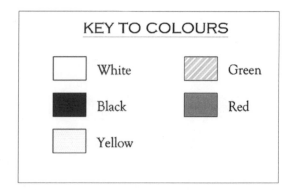

KEY TO COLOURS

White

Green

Black

Red

Yellow

use a horizontal arm to indicate 'stop' (or 'danger' in railway parlance); the arms of upper quadrant semaphores move upwards through 45 degrees to indicate 'proceed' (or 'clear'), while lower quadrant signal arms move downwards through the same angle.

Distant signals work in the same way but a horizontal arm means 'caution', indicating that the driver should expect to see a home signal at 'danger' ahead. Semaphore signals are fitted with coloured lenses to show a green light for 'line clear' at night or a red lamp for 'danger' (home signals) or yellow lamp for 'caution' (distant signals). See the diagrams on the previous pages for details on signals. Semaphore signals are controlled from closely spaced signal boxes.

Modern signalling uses four-aspect colour light signalling due to the higher speeds attained by modern trains. Once a route is set up from a modern 'power box', which can be many miles from the signals and points (see p.158) it controls, the signals are controlled automatically by the passage of trains through track circuits. A green signal means that a train can proceed at full line speed as the line is clear for at least three more signals; two amber lights mean that the signal after next is at danger and the train should reduce speed, a single amber indication shows that the next signal is at danger, meaning the train must prepare to stop, and a red lamp means that the section of track behind the signal is occupied by another train and the approaching train must stop.

Pocket Fact

Many of today's smaller preserved railways do not have any physical mechanical signals, relying on a principle known as 'One Engine in Steam' which dates from the earliest days of signalling. This rule means that only one train can be in use on a single line at any one time, and this way the risk of collisions is eliminated without the need for actual signals.

⊞⊞⊞ MOVING THE MAIL: ⊞⊞⊞
THE TRAVELLING POST OFFICE

The railways carried the mail from their earliest days. Mail often contained items of value and as it was susceptible to theft when carried by road, the railways provided a fast and secure way of transporting it. Initially, previously sorted mail was carried but in 1838, mail was sorted on a train as it went along, which sped up the postal service considerably. The Great Western Railway became the first railway to run special mail trains in February 1855 and these spread to other railways throughout the country. These trains became known as the Travelling Post Office (usually abbreviated to TPO), and things improved further in 1866 when the Great Western Railway introduced apparatus that enabled mail to be picked up and set down from a fast-moving train. Similar apparatus was used throughout the country until the 1970s when its use was discontinued. However, mail is still moved by rail in Britain, and some new 4-car EMUs were delivered in 1995 and can be seen travelling from London to Glasgow and Edinburgh at speeds of up to 100mph.

Pocket Fact 🖂

The biggest mail train robbery took place in 1963, when thieves held up the Glasgow to London TPO train in Bedfordshire. They got away with £2.6 million in cash, the equivalent of an astonishing £40 million today. Most of the gang of 15 robbers were caught, including Ronnie Biggs and 'Buster' Edwards. The robbery was immortalised in the movie Buster *in 1988.*

2

THE TRAINS
THEMSELVES

So far we've talked about trains, engines and locomotives, but what's the difference? How do they work? What are the advantages and disadvantages of the various forms of power? All will become clear in this chapter.

⪢ TECHNICAL TERMS ⪡
EXPLAINED

Firstly, what is a train? Modern trains can take many forms, but in simple terms a train traditionally consists of a number of passenger carriages (also called coaches) or freight wagons (sometimes called trucks) pulled by a locomotive.

LOCOMOTIVES

The name 'locomotive' was coined by George Stephenson to describe his self-powered steam engine, but is now applied to any self-contained power unit used to haul a train. They are often miscalled 'engines'; although an engine is only one part of a locomotive.

STEAM LOCOMOTIVES

Steam locomotives consist of a boiler (see p.47), which is partly filled with water. A fire, contained in a firebox attached to one end of the boiler, heats the water to produce steam, which fills the space in the boiler not taken up by the water. As the boiler is sealed, the steam can be held at very high pressure. It is then used to drive the 'engine' part of the locomotive, which consists of two or more cylinders. The steam is directed into the cylinders by valves, which control the direction and gearing of the engine, and then drives a piston in each cylinder, that in turn drives a rod connected to a crank on the wheels or driving axles (see the diagram on p.45).

Steam locomotives made use of coal, an abundant fuel in Britain, and so were cheap to run until fuel oils became more widely available. However, they are less efficient and more labour-intensive than diesel or electric locomotives. Steam locomotives often tow a special wagon, containing the necessary coal and water to generate the steam for their journey. This wagon is referred to as a tender. Others carry their water in tanks and their coal in a bunker either on the back of the cab or inside the cab itself; these are called tank locomotives. See pp44–61 for more on steam locomotives.

Pocket Fact 🚂

Tank locomotives can be further divided into several types. Side Tank locomotives carry a water tank low down on either side of the boiler, while Pannier Tanks, favoured by the Great Western Railway, carry similar tanks higher up on the boiler with a gap between the boiler and the wheels. Saddle Tanks, as their name suggests, carry a single tank that sits on top of the boiler like a saddle, curving around either side, and Well Tanks have one or more tanks low down between the chassis frames.

DIESEL MECHANICAL LOCOMOTIVES

Diesel mechanical locomotives first appeared on the main lines of Britain in the 1930s, and examples of this type (including the British Railways Class 03 and 04) were built until the 1960s. However, mechanical transmission is unsuitable for high speed running and heavy haulage, and other methods had to be found for larger express locomotives. Many types of Diesel Multiple Unit (DMU; see pp40 and 168) also use mechanical transmission.

DIESEL ELECTRIC LOCOMOTIVES

Diesel electric locomotives use a diesel engine to drive an electricity generator, which in turn feeds power to a series of traction motors that drive the axles. This method of transmission is still common today, as locomotives of this type can be both fast and powerful. The disadvantage of this type of drive is that all the equipment needed makes the locomotives heavy. This resulted in some of the early British Railways diesels, such as the Class 31s, 40s and 45s, needing extra carrying wheels to distribute the weight (see p.63).

DIESEL HYDRAULIC LOCOMOTIVES

Diesel hydraulic locomotives appeared on the Western Region of British Railways in 1958, though they had been successfully used in Germany some years before. This type of locomotive used one or more diesel engines to drive a 'torque converter', which is similar to an automatic gearbox in a car. This then drives the axles of the rail wheels. The ensemble is light and powerful, but requires more specialist equipment to maintain it than a diesel electric locomotive of similar power.

ELECTRIC LOCOMOTIVES

Electric locomotives are used to haul some of today's fastest trains, though many modern ones are actually Electric Multiple Units (EMUs; see pp40 and 169). The trunk routes of the East Coast Main Line from King's Cross to Edinburgh and the West Coast Main Line between Euston and Glasgow Central, together with some lines in East Anglia and some minor lines, are electrified using an overhead wire system called catenary (see pp29–30), and the electricity is collected for the train by a pantograph. The mass of lines that make up the suburban commuter network to the south of London, and some railways in and around Liverpool, are electrified using a third rail. This extra rail located on insulating pots on the ends of the sleepers outside the running rails carries the electricity supply, which is collected by means of a shoe on the train (see the illustration on pp27–29). The fourth rail system (see pp26 and 28) used by London Underground is similar to third rail but has an extra rail located between the running rails to carry the return current. Electric trains are fast, efficient, quiet and clean in use but the infrastructure is very expensive to install initially.

Pocket Fact

Electric locomotives normally collect their power supply from an outside source, such as a third rail or an overhead wire. However, some special locomotives, such as those used for engineering works on London's underground railways, are battery powered.

MULTIPLE UNITS

Multiple Units are commonplace on today's railways; well-known British examples include the Pendolino (see p.70) and Voyager (see p.68) used on the West Coast Main Line. While there are many detail differences between the types, the main distinction between them is whether they are powered by diesel engines (referred to as DMUs) or electric motors (EMUs). A multiple unit consists of one or more powered carriages (which are called 'cars'). A driving cab is fitted at the outer ends of the unit, and two or more units may be coupled together and the train controlled as one from the leading cab. EMUs have motors driving some or all of the axles, while in the case of DMUs the engines may be slung underneath (as on the Voyagers) or inside the cars (as in the High Speed Trains used in the west of England). The type of transmission used on modern trains may be diesel mechanical (only the Class 121s, and Classes 142–144 'Pacers' remain of this type; see p.38), diesel electric (as on the High Speed Trains and Voyagers), or diesel hydraulic (on most commuter trains including the 'Sprinters' of classes 150–159 and express units like the Class 180 Adelante; see p.39). Some DMUs and EMUs were built (or converted from redundant passenger units) specifically to carry mail; see p.36).

Weather

We've all heard the jokes about the 'wrong kind of snow' and 'leaves on the line', but the weather really does cause problems for trains, particularly where their electricity is supplied by a third rail.

Snow can completely cover a third rail, and when it gets compacted or iced firm it can prevent the current from being collected properly. On all lines, compacted snow and ice can stop points changing, meaning that some routes can't be set until the snow is cleared.

Leaf fall causes problems during autumn because when leaves fall on the line and get crushed by train wheels they produce a greasy mulch. This then prevents a train's wheels from gripping, and this means they have difficulty in starting from rest, climbing hills and, most importantly, stopping. This isn't a new phenomenon, but was kept at bay during steam days by cutting back the trees so that leaves couldn't fall on the line. These days, lineside maintenance is a shadow of its former self and trees grow in abundance, meaning the leaf fall on the rails is significantly greater.

CARRIAGES AND WAGONS

The term 'rolling stock' is used to describe the vehicles that move on a railway, including locomotives, multiple units, carriages (those with bogies, see pp42 and 168, are normally referred to as coaches or 'coaching stock') and wagons. However, locomotives are sometimes classified separately as 'motive power' or 'running stock', and the term 'rolling stock' is then used to refer just to coaches and wagons.

Railway carriage development

In the earliest days of the railways, passenger carriages were usually nothing more than open-topped wagons, but things soon progressed. Even in the early days of the Liverpool & Manchester Railway there were three classes of passenger travel; the bulk of passengers travelled in third-class carriages, which were open to the elements and had no seating – they were basically open-topped wagons. Those of slightly better means travelled second-class, in a covered carriage but on hard wooden seats, while only the wealthiest could afford to travel first-class, in relatively plush and enclosed surroundings in what were effectively stage coaches on rails. All of the coaches had only four wheels and rudimentary suspension, giving a very rough ride compared with modern coaches, but they were a vast improvement on the stage coaches of the day.

Improvements were made gradually and by the 1850s all carriages were fully enclosed; six wheels became commonplace on passenger stock in the 1860s, giving a better ride, and gas lighting was introduced during the same period. Heating was introduced by passing steam from the locomotives into metal pipes, which acted as radiators, in the carriages. Sleeping cars (see p.171) first appeared in America in 1865, with Britain following suit in the 1870s. Continuous brakes (see p.168) began to appear in the same decade which were applied from the locomotive and worked on every vehicle in the train, providing smoother braking and preventing trains from running away. If coaches became detached because a coupling broke the brakes would automatically stop the whole train, including the detached portion.

Pocket Fact 🐝

In 1874, the Midland Railway introduced the first bogie coaches in Britain. Bogies are basically 4-wheeled trucks mounted on pivots at each end of a passenger coach (and also on some modern freight wagons). They remove unevenness in the track, giving a smooth ride, and also allow coaches to be made longer as they can still fit round tight curves without binding.

Over the 50 years following the introduction of the bogie, the coach evolved more or less into the vehicle we recognise today. The longer coaches allowed the introduction of compartments containing six or eight seats; the use of different compartment standards allowed different passenger classes to travel in one coach (known as a 'composite'). Corridors were added to allow passengers and staff to move between compartments, and corridor connections, which allowed passengers to move between coaches, appeared shortly afterwards.

The first lavatories appeared on trains in 1882, and second-class accommodation was discontinued in the late 19th century (except on some boat trains; see pp106–108), again with the Midland Railway leading the way and others following suit. The comfort of third-class was raised to the level of second-class at the same time (though second-class, now referred to as 'Standard Class', returned in 1956 under British Railways when third-class was abolished). Restaurant cars (sometimes referred to as dining cars) were introduced at the start of the 20th century.

Modern coaches have open saloons rather than separate compartments, and the seats are much closer together than on many older coaches, with a large proportion of seats arranged in 'airline' pattern (all forward or rearward facing with fold-down trays on the seat backs) rather than around tables. This means more passengers can be carried per vehicle, increasing profitability. Most trains now have automatic doors, which saves time and cost at stations as there is now no need for a guard to physically check doors are closed before the train departs.

Wagons

The movement of goods was the principal reason the railways were invented, and millions of goods wagons (the term 'trucks' is no longer used) were built over the years to carry virtually every type of traffic imaginable. The early 'chaldron' wagons were replaced by short 4-wheeled open wagons, while perishable goods were conveyed in enclosed vans. The underframes (the wagon chassis) were originally made of wood, but later made of steel girders, and the wagon and van bodies were constructed from wooden planks (though steel wagons and hoppers appeared in the 1930s). Livestock such as cattle and horses travelled in specially built wagons, and milk, petrol and oil were transported in 4- or 6-wheeled tankers.

The design of these wagons remained unchanged in Britain for over a century, until bogie wagons and tankers began to appear in the 1960s. Until recently, most goods rolling stock did not have a continuous brake (these were known as unfitted wagons; see p.172), and each wagon was fitted instead with a handbrake. These required a train to stop before descending a steep hill so that the individual brakes on each wagon could be applied to prevent them running away downhill. A special heavy wagon called a brake van brought up the rear of an unfitted train, and contained accommodation for the guard (see p.167) and an adjustable handbrake he could apply from inside the vehicle.

⊞⊞⊞ STEAM LOCOMOTIVES ⊞⊞⊞

Steam locomotives held sway in Britain for 130 years, and as trains got longer and heavier the locomotives became larger and more powerful. Boilers became bigger so that they could generate more steam, and more wheels were needed to distribute the extra weight. In Britain, Whyte Notation (devised by Frederick Methvan Whyte in the early 20th century) is used to describe locomotives by the wheel arrangement: the first number denotes the number of weight-carrying wheels at the front of the locomotive, the second gives the number of driving wheels and the third gives the number of trailing wheels.

Pocket Fact 🚂

The driving wheels of a steam locomotive are those that are powered by connecting rods from the pistons (often described as driven wheels); more driving wheels can be added by joining them together with coupling rods (see the diagram opposite).

DRIVING WHEELS

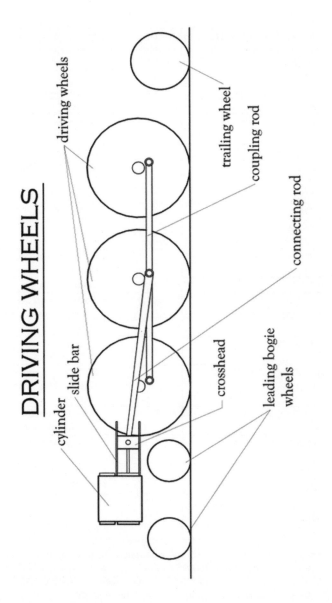

cylinder

slide bar

driving wheels

trailing wheel

coupling rod

connecting rod

crosshead

leading bogie wheels

WHYTE NOTATION			
Side view of locomotive (front to the left)	Whyte Notation description	Notation name (if used in the UK)	Famous locomotives of the type
Oo	0-2-2	Northumbrian	Northumbrian
oO	2-2-0		Rocket, Planet
oOo	2-2-2		North Star, Fire Fly
ooOo	4-2-2		Midland Railway 673
OO	0-4-0		Locomotion No 1
oOO	2-4-0		Well tanks 30585 and 30587
OOo	0-4-2		Lion, GWR 14XX
oOOo	2-4-2		L&Y 1008
ooOO	4-4-0		City of Truro
ooOOo	4-4-2	Atlantic	Henry Oakley
OOO	0-6-0		GWR 'Pannier Tanks', LMS '4F'
OOOo	0-6-2		Gresley 'N2' class
oOOO	2-6-0	Mogul	'Pocket Rocket' 76079
oOOOo	2-6-2	Prairie	GWR Large and Small Prairie Tanks
oOOOoo	2-6-4		BR Standard and LMS Fairburn Tanks
ooOOO	4-6-0		GWR 'Kings' and 'Castles', LMS 'Royal Scots'
ooOOOo	4-6-2	Pacific	Flying Scotsman, Tornado, Mallard
ooOOOoo	4-6-4		Gresley's W1 'Hush Hush'
OOOO	0-8-0		'Super D' 49351
oOOOO	2-8-0		LMS '8F's
oOOOOo	2-8-2	Mikado	Gresley P2s
OOOOO	0-10-0		
oOOOOO	2-10-0		BR 9Fs, Evening Star

Notes: Tank engines bore a suffix denoting the type, eg 2-6-4T for a side tank locomotive, 0-6-0ST for a saddle tank locomotive, 0-6-0PT for a pannier tank and 2-4-0WT for a well tank (see p.172). Those without a suffix would normally have a tender.

THE STEAM LOCOMOTIVE DEVELOPS

In many ways the steam locomotive we know today is still a clear ancestor of Stephenson's *Rocket*: a coal fire in the firebox produces steam in the boiler, and this then drives pistons within two or more cylinders that provide power to the driving wheels.

However, there are some significant differences. Even in Victorian times, trains were becoming very heavy and were sometimes pulled by two locomotives (known as double heading) or more, which was expensive in terms of crews and locomotive wear. As boiler making techniques improved, boilers were made that were capable of holding steam at a higher pressure. The higher the pressure of the steam, the more power could be extracted from it. *Rocket*, for example, had a boiler pressure of just 50 pounds per square inch (abbreviated to psi), and the replica locomotive recently constructed struggles to start itself on a gradient, even without a train attached. Oliver Bulleid's 'Merchant Navy' class had a boiler pressure of an incredible 280psi when built; though most locomotives have boiler pressures in the range of between 180psi–250psi, there were some experimental ones built with very high pressures.

High pressure experiments

In 1929, both the LMS and LNER railways experimented with high pressure boilers, each producing a prototype to test the theory of their greater efficiency.

The LNER locomotive, W1 10000 was nicknamed 'Hush Hush' due to the secrecy surrounding its construction. It used a ship-type boiler with a pressure of 450psi, and used a compound (see p.49) arrangement for the cylinders, with two low-pressure ones on the outside and a high-pressure one between the frames. Its unusual boiler profile, unlike anything seen before, led to its other nickname 'The Galloping Sausage'. It was unsuccessful as it was found to be less efficient than normal steam locomotives of a similar size. It was rebuilt in 1936 with a standard-type boiler similar to those used on the streamlined A4 class (see p.52), though it retained its unique 4-6-4 wheel arrangement, making it the only British standard gauge tender locomotive to use it.

The LMS locomotive, 6399 *Fury*, used the chassis of a conventional Royal Scot class locomotive (see p.54) and compounding (see below) married to a special boiler that produced both high-pressure steam at 900psi and low-pressure steam at 250psi. A special sealed ultra-high pressure circuit (that could be likened to a combi-boilered central heating system in a house) was used to transmit heat from the firebox through tubes into the high-pressure boiler. These tubes worked at an incredible 1800psi, and during testing in 1930 one of these burst, killing a man who was on the footplate. *Fury* was repaired and testing continued, but again it was unsuccessful and inefficient. It was rebuilt in 1935, becoming the first of the 'Rebuilt Scot' class (see p.54), 6170 *British Legion*.

Superheating

Even before these high pressure experiments were thought of, another way of increasing the efficiency of steam was developed by Wilhelm Schmidt in Germany in the late 1880s. Superheating was one of the most important advances in steam locomotive technology, and was first applied in Britain by the Great Western Railway in 1906.

A superheater is a system of tubes within a locomotive boiler that is used to increase the efficiency of the steam. Instead of taking the steam generated in the boiler straight to the cylinders, it is collected in the superheater header and taken via a system of tubes (called superheater elements) back through some large tubes called superheater flues in the boiler and heated further. The resultant superheated steam has much more energy than that which comes directly from the boiler (which is referred to as saturated steam).

Pocket Fact

The driver of the Hogwarts Express trains during the filming of the Harry Potter movies was West Coast Railways driver Bill Andrew, who retired at the end of 2010 after 60 years working with steam trains. For the Harry Potter films, the fireman of the Hogwarts Express was often Frank Santrian, widely recognised as one of the finest 'gentlemen of the footplate', who retired in 2009 at the age of 75.

COMPOUND LOCOMOTIVES

Another theoretical way of increasing the efficiency of a steam locomotive is that of compounding. In a normal locomotive, steam is fed separately to each cylinder and then exhausted through the blastpipe (see p.167) and chimney to the atmosphere. In a compound locomotive, the steam is first fed into one or more high pressure cylinders and then fed into low pressure cylinders before being exhausted. The system dates back to the stationary engines in mills before the Victorian era but was first applied to locomotives in America in the 1850s. Francis Webb introduced the first compound locomotive in Britain in 1878, but arguably the most famous is Midland Compound 1000, preserved in the National Collection. This was built in 1902 by the Midland Railway and was rebuilt with a superheater in 1914. The design was so successful that almost identical examples were being built into 1932, and survived until the end of the 1950s.

ARTICULATED LOCOMOTIVES

On lines with sharp curves and steep gradients, very powerful but agile locomotives are needed. Those with lots of driving wheels on a straight chassis are unable to go around sharp curves as the flanges (see p.169) bind on the rails. The answer lay in mounting the boiler, cab and coal and water supplies on a separate frame and then adding two engine units (containing the chassis, wheels and cylinders) underneath on pivots, producing an articulated locomotive, of which there are several types.

Double Fairlie

These are almost two locomotives in one; a central cab and firebox has an identical boiler, smokebox and pair of side tanks emerging in front and behind, and a 4-wheeled 'power bogie', with all wheels driven, under each end with the cylinders facing outwards. It was invented by Robert Fairlie, and the idea was patented in 1864. The surviving examples are narrow gauge, but can be found in regular use on the Ffestiniog Railway in Wales. A new locomotive identical in design was built in 1992, and the railway has three of the type in regular use, plus a Single Fairlie which is effectively half a double one with just one boiler and power bogie, with trailing wheels under the cab.

Garratt

In 1907, Herbert William Garratt invented a fully articulated locomotive that worked in a similar way to Robert Fairlie's design but was much more capable, powerful and smooth-riding. Unlike Fairlie's locomotive, the Garratt had a single boiler mounted in the centre of a frame with a cab and coal space at one end over one power bogie and a water tank over the other. The design was further improved by manufacturers Beyer, Peacock shortly afterwards and the locomotives became known as Beyer Garratts. Many hundreds were built, and though the first ones were built to narrow gauge, standard gauge ones were supplied to the LMS (33 locomotives) and the LNER (a single example). In Britain, the only ones currently operational are on the Welsh Highland Railway. Like the Fairlie locomotives, the cylinders face outwards but carrying wheels are often used, again at the outward ends. Whyte Notation considers them as two locomotives coupled back-to-back; as an example the LMS ones were described as 2-6-0+0-6-2, the '+' denoting the articulation.

Mallet

Mallet locomotives are similar to Garratts in that they have two power units under the boiler, cab and coal and water spaces, but they differ in that the rear unit is fixed to the main frame containing the boiler and only the front unit pivots. The cylinders on each unit normally face forwards, and the coal and water could sometimes be carried in a separate tender. This type of locomotive was not used in Britain, but was initially quite popular in America. The Union Pacific 'Big Boy' was a 2-8-8-4 (ie two leading wheels, two sets of eight driving wheels and four trailing wheels) was one of the largest locomotives of this type.

‖‖‖‖ FAMOUS STEAM ‖‖‖‖ LOCOMOTIVES

FLYING SCOTSMAN

Number and name: 4472 *Flying Scotsman*

Class: A3 (originally A1)

Wheel arrangement: 4-6-2

Number of cylinders: 3 (2 outside the frames, 1 between the frames)

Designer: Sir Nigel Gresley

Railway of origin: London & North Eastern Railway

Year introduced: 1923

History: Built as 'un-named 1472' in 1923 *Flying Scotsman* is reputed to be the world's most famous steam locomotive. It acquired its name and new number when it was exhibited at the 1924 British Empire Exhibition in Wembley, and was selected to launch the prestigious non-stop 'Flying Scotsman' express in 1928. In 1934 it became the first locomotive to officially reach 100mph during test runs, but its design was outdated even then and it was rebuilt as an improved A3 class in 1947, just before it became the property of British Railways. With the end of steam approaching *Flying Scotsman* was withdrawn in 1963 and preserved by Alan Pegler. It then returned to use, hauling many railtours on lines where other steam locomotives had long disappeared, until 1969 when it went to the USA on tour. Financial difficulties saw the locomotive change hands and return to the UK, where it resumed traffic once again. *Flying Scotsman* travelled to Australia in 1988 in connection with the country's bi-centenary celebrations, and while there it set a non-stop distance world record for steam traction of 442 miles (711 km) that stands to this day. Back in the UK once more, it became the property of the National Railway Museum in 2004, and began a full overhaul and restoration in 2007. It was relaunched into service in May 2011.

Where can I see it?: *Flying Scotsman* will be in frequent action on the main line, but will also visit a number of heritage lines throughout the country, including the East Lancashire Railway in Bury near Manchester. Its home base will be the National Railway Museum in York.

MALLARD

Number and name: 4468 *Mallard*

Class: A4

Wheel arrangement: 4-6-2

Number of cylinders: 3 (2 outside the frames, 1 between the frames)

Designer: Sir Nigel Gresley

Railway of origin: London & North Eastern Railway

Year introduced: 1938

History: *Mallard* is officially the fastest steam locomotive in the world, setting its record of 126mph (203km/h) on 3 July 1930. It is one of six of its class preserved, but is currently the only one restored to original condition, in LNER blue with side skirts (called valances) over the wheels. On passing into British Railways ownership in 1948 it was renumbered 60022, and was preserved on withdrawal in 1963, passing into the National Collection in light of its historical significance. It made a brief return to steam in 1986 but since 1988 it has been on static display. Fortunately, there are several of the class either under overhaul or active in preservation, including 60007 *Sir Nigel Gresley*, 60009 *Union of South Africa* and 60019 *Bittern*.

Where can I see it?: *Mallard* normally resides at the National Railway Museum in York but moved for a short stay at Locomotion, Shildon, in 2010 while renovations took place at York. If you can't get to see it, 60007 is based on the North Yorkshire Moors Railway, and both it and 60019 appear regularly on the main line around Britain hauling special charter trains. 60008 *Dwight D. Eisenhower* is on display at the National Railroad

Museum, Wisconsin, USA and 60010 *Dominion of Canada* is located at the Canadian Railway Museum.

ROCKET

Number and name: *Rocket*

Class: None

Wheel arrangement: 0-2-2

Number of cylinders: 2, outside the frames

Designers: George and Robert Stephenson

Railway of origin: Liverpool & Manchester Railway

Year introduced: 1829

History: The outright winner of the Rainhill Trials, *Rocket* may not have been the first steam locomotive as is often thought, but it helped secure George and Robert Stephenson's place in history as the finest railway engineers of their day. Its boiler was a departure from everything that had gone before and modern steam locomotives still use a similar design. When originally built, its cylinders were mounted at an angle of 35 degrees to the horizontal. Previously, all locomotives had used vertically mounted cylinders (Stephenson's *Locomotion No 1* is a good example) but this made them unstable at speed, and *Rocket*'s design improved this. It was soon modified to have the cylinders mounted almost horizontally, a design still used to this day. It is in this form that the locomotive was preserved; it was donated to the Patent Office in 1862.

Where can I see it?: The original *Rocket* still exists as a static exhibit at the Science Museum in London, but is scarcely recognisable compared to drawings of the locomotive that took part in the Rainhill Trials. A replica, with sections cut away to show its construction, is on display at the National Railway Museum, York, and a working replica was constructed for the National Railway Museum in 2010 and has toured the heritage lines of the UK.

ROYAL SCOT

Number and name: 6100 *Royal Scot*

Class: Rebuilt Scot

Wheel arrangement: 4-6-0

Number of cylinders: 3 (2 outside the frames, 1 between the frames)

Designer: Henry Fowler, modified by Sir William Stanier

Railway of origin: London Midland & Scottish Railway

Year introduced: 1927

History: *Royal Scot* was one of the first large locomotives built by the LMS; previously when more power was required, trains would be double-headed. The locomotive was successful and was selected to tour America in 1933. When originally built, the class of 70 locomotives had parallel-sided boilers but rebuilding began during the Second World War when the boilers and cylinders began to wear out, and tapered boilers were eventually added to all the class, with *Royal Scot* being so converted in 1950. *Royal Scot* was preserved by Billy Butlin in 1962 as an exhibit for his Skegness Holiday Camp before being restored at Bressingham Steam Museum in 1972. After a period of seven years in steam it remained as a static exhibit until 2009 when its overhaul was deemed complete and a brief stint in traffic occurred. Major faults were found shortly afterwards and the locomotive was again stripped down; a return to the main line was due in 2011.

Where can I see it?: *Royal Scot* will be active on the main line for several years, but is likely to be based at Southall, London, for much of the time. Visits to heritage lines are very likely, and these will be detailed in the railway press (see pp147–148) as details are announced. Another member of the class, 46115 *Scots Guardsman*, has also been preserved and is operated on the main line by West Coast Railways; its base is at Carnforth in north-west England.

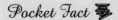

Pocket Fact

What isn't well known is that when Royal Scot *was selected to tour America the LMS decided against sending their prized locomotive overseas in case any harm befell it; instead 6100* Royal Scot *swapped identities with 6152* The King's Dragoon Guardsman; *however on its return from America the identities were never swapped back.*

CITY OF TRURO

Number and name: 3717 (originally 3440) *City of Truro*

Class: 37XX 'City'

Wheel arrangement: 4-4-0

Number of cylinders: 2, inside the frames

Designer: George Jackson Churchward

Railway of origin: Great Western Railway

Year introduced: 1903

History: *City of Truro* is credited with being the first locomotive to reach a speed of 100mph (160km/h), while descending Wellington Bank in Somerset at the head of the 'Ocean Mails' Plymouth to London special train in 1904. However, the speed was not officially recorded but timed by on-train observers between distance posts. The Great Western Railway originally wanted the speed played down so as not to be seen as having been reckless, but the fact ended up in the newspapers shortly afterwards and the locomotive's place in history was assured. It was rebuilt with a superheated boiler in 1911 and renumbered 3717 in 1912, eventually being preserved upon withdrawal in 1931. It has been overhauled and used a number of times, and was most recently returned to traffic in 2004 for the 100th anniversary of its 100mph run. It is still operational, now part of the National Collection and owned by the National Railway Museum.

Where can I see it?: *City of Truro* regularly visits heritage railways and is currently based on the Gloucestershire Warwickshire Railway at Toddington. It is always in demand for steam galas and events countrywide, so check before you travel to see it.

TORNADO

Number and name: 60163 *Tornado*

Class: A1

Wheel arrangement: 4-6-2

Number of cylinders: 3 (2 outside the frames, 1 between the frames)

Designer: Arthur Peppercorn

Railway of origin: London & North Eastern Railway/British Railways

Year introduced: 2008

History: *Tornado* is probably the most famous steam locomotive in operation in Britain today, despite the fact it is almost 50 years newer than the last standard gauge main line locomotive built for Britain's railways. The A1 class was designed under the auspices of the LNER, but the first one was not delivered until after the railways had been nationalised. Between 1948 and 1949, 49 of the class were built, but, despite a design-life of around 40 years, all had been scrapped by 1966. The idea for *Tornado* was formed in the late 1980s and in 1990, the A1 Steam Locomotive Trust was formed to collect subscriptions from supporters in order to amass funds to build a new A1. The build took 18 years but the locomotive was completed in 2008, taking its first main line passenger train in January 2009. It has a huge following, drawing crowds wherever it goes.

Where can I see it?: *Tornado* travels the length and breadth of the country, both on main line tours and to heritage railways. It is in operation most weekends and many weekdays too, so if you check the railway press (see pp147–148) you are sure to find it at a station near you.

DUCHESS OF HAMILTON

Number and name: 6229 *Duchess of Hamilton*

Class: Princess Coronation

Wheel arrangement: 4-6-2

Number of cylinders: 4 (2 outside the frames, 2 between the frames)

Designer: Sir William Stanier

Railway of origin: London Midland & Scottish Railway

Year introduced: 1938

History: *Duchess of Hamilton* is the only surviving streamlined locomotive from the LMS railway, but the streamlined shape is perhaps not as sleek as that applied to the A4s. This was because the LMS needed power as well as speed and fitted the largest boiler they possibly could; the streamlined casing was really an afterthought. Nonetheless the Princess Coronations (or 'Duchesses' as they are often called) were highly successful, briefly holding the British speed record of 114mph until it was broken by *Mallard*. Like *Royal Scot* before it, class namesake 6220 *Coronation* was asked to travel to America to appear at the New York World's Fair in 1939. Yet again, the LMS decided against sending their prized locomotive and performed an identity swap with *Duchess of Hamilton*, sending the latter instead. While the 'Duchess' was in the USA, war broke out, leaving the locomotive stranded until the LMS finally decided to risk bringing it home in 1942. Unlike *Royal Scot*, the identities (name and number on the locomotive itself) of *Coronation* and *Duchess of Hamilton* were swapped back in 1943. The 'Duchess' had its streamlining removed in 1947. Upon withdrawal from British Railways, it was purchased by Billy Butlin and displayed at Minehead Holiday Camp until 1976. It was then placed in the custody of the National Collection, for which it was eventually purchased in 1987. It returned to the main line for two spells of charter work until 1996, after which the locomotive has remained a static exhibit. Its streamlining was restored in 2009.

Where can I see it?: *Duchess of Hamilton* currently resides at the National Railway Museum in York. Two other members of the class are also preserved, 46235 *City of Birmingham* at the Think Tank museum, Birmingham, and 6233 *Duchess of Sutherland* at the Midland Railway, Butterley, though the latter is currently dismantled for a full overhaul. Neither of the latter two is streamlined.

CLAN LINE

Number and name: 35028 *Clan Line* ('Venice-Simplon Orient Express' locomotive)

Class: Rebuilt Merchant Navy

Wheel arrangement: 4-6-2

Number of cylinders: 3 (2 outside the frames, 1 between the frames)

Designer: Oliver Vaughan Snell Bulleid

Railway of origin: Southern Railway/British Railways

Year introduced: 1948 (rebuilt 1959–1960)

History: *Clan Line* is one of 30 original members of the 'Merchant Navy' class built between 1941 and 1949 for the Southern Railway (later the Southern Region of British Railways). Wartime restrictions on building passenger locomotives were avoided by describing the class as 'mixed traffic' (ie for pulling freight and passenger trains) which they clearly were not. When built, the locomotives had a flat streamlined or 'air-smoothed' casing around the boiler, and the valve gear was driven by a chain mechanism between the frames. While the locomotives were very powerful, the chain-driven valve gear was problematic and the air-smoothed casing prevented access to the workings for maintenance. When crank axles (those fastened to the rod from the middle cylinder) began to fail the entire class was withdrawn for rebuilding, involving the removal of the casing, fitting of conventional valve gear and the fitting of smoke deflectors (see p.171). *Clan Line* was the last to be rebuilt, emerging from Eastleigh Works in 1960, but it was withdrawn just seven years later, being purchased straight from BR by the Merchant Navy Locomotive Preservation Society Ltd. *Clan Line* is currently operational, but 10 other members of the class survive in various stages of repair from scrapyard condition to display status.

Where can I see it?: *Clan Line* is regularly used to pull the Venice-Simplon Orient Express (VSOE) dining trains (see pp110–111) from London Victoria and Waterloo to a number of destinations in the south-east of England. Sadly, it works very few other trains, so your best bet to see it is to look on the UK Steam website (see p.135) and watch it from the lineside.

HOGWARTS CASTLE/OLTON HALL

Number and name: 5972 *Hogwarts Castle* (normally *Olton Hall*)

Class: Hall

Wheel arrangement: 4-6-0

Number of cylinders: 2, outside the frames

Designer: Charles B. Collett

Railway of origin: Great Western Railway

Year introduced: 1937

History: *Olton Hall* was just one of 11 survivors of a class of 259 locomotives built at Swindon Works (see p.83) between 1928 and 1943. In contrast to many other famous locomotives, its original career was pretty ordinary, with little happening to it before its withdrawal from British Railways in 1963, after which it went to the famous Barry Scrapyard in South Wales, where it languished until 1981. Its claim to fame came in 2000 when it was repainted from its normal green colour into maroon and had the Hogwarts crest applied (from the Hogwarts School of Witchcraft and Wizardry in the Harry Potter series). Since then it has appeared in all the Harry Potter films and is also in demand for special fan rail charters.

Where can I see it?: *Olton Hall/Hogwarts Castle* is based at West Coast Railways' depot at Carnforth in Lancashire. The depot is not accessible to the public, and the best way of seeing the locomotive is to look out for it on a main line railtour; a list of these is available on the UK Steam website (see p.135).

Pocket Fact 🎟

5972 Olton Hall *isn't the only locomotive to have been repainted and re-named to represent Hogwarts Castle. The first one to be so treated was a rebuilt Bulleid 'West Country' class, 34027* Taw Valley, *which was used to promote the fourth book in the series. Rebuilt into its current shape in 1957, its appearance was considered to be too modern for the films.*

DUKE OF GLOUCESTER

Number and name: 71000 *Duke of Gloucester*

Class: BR Standard Class 8

Wheel arrangement: 4-6-2

Number of cylinders: 3 (2 outside the frames, 1 between the frames)

Designer: Robert Riddles

Railway of origin: British Railways

Year introduced: 1954

History: *Duke of Gloucester* was the prototype for a planned new class of express passenger locomotive, but was destined to remain a one-off. It had a large boiler and Caprotti valve gear (which works similar to valves in a car engine) which should have made it the most powerful locomotive of its type, but it was dogged with problems. It was branded a 'poor steamer' by crews, and lacked the power and efficiency it should have exhibited. As a result it was quietly sent for scrap after a working life of just eight years, but was rescued from Barry Scrapyard by a group of enthusiasts that would evolve into today's 71000 Trust. They set about restoring it, and in doing so they found and rectified many manufacturing and design faults, resulting in *Duke of Gloucester* being one of today's finest main line performers.

Where can I see it?: *Duke of Gloucester* is based at the East Lancashire Railway in Bury near Manchester. The locomotive can often be seen pulling trains on the line, but is also very active on the main line pulling special trains and is a popular visitor at gala events on other heritage railways.

⁂ DAWN OF THE DIESELS ⁂

While diesel railcars and multiple units had been used on some secondary services and in shunting yards from the 1930s, they didn't challenge steam's supremacy on Britain's main lines until after the Second World War.

Diesel engines developed significantly during the war and in December 1947 the LMS introduced 10000, the first main line diesel electric locomotive. Its power plant, electricity generator and traction motors (the electric motors that drove the wheels) were forerunners of those used in many British Railways diesel types. It was designed to have a power rating similar to that of a 'Black 5', which was a medium-sized mixed traffic steam locomotive of the time, so it wasn't powerful enough to pull the heavy, fast expresses on its own.

To do this, another identical locomotive, 10001, was finished in 1948 by British Railways, and the pair would double-head the expresses. While they were successful, progress on developing the diesel engine was swift and they were out of date in less than 10 years, lasting only until the mid-1960s before withdrawal. Nonetheless, they were the shape of things to come, and the Southern Region of British Railways introduced three similar prototypes using progressively more powerful versions of the same diesel engine.

Originally, diesel engines were heavy, and it wasn't always possible to put a traction motor on every axle; sometimes, just like with steam locomotives, extra carrying wheels had to be added to distribute the weight and avoid damaging track and structures.

DESCRIBING THE NEW DIESELS

Diesel wheel arrangements are described using the British version of the UIC Classification system. Letters are used to describe the number of consecutively powered axles, with A for one powered axle, B for two, C for three, and so on. To denote a bogie with axles individually driven by traction motors, a lower-case letter 'o' is used, and the number of consecutive unpowered axles is denoted by a number. It sounds complicated, but it really isn't, as the table on p.63 shows.

THE 'PILOT SCHEME'

In 1955, British Railways took the decision to modernise Britain's railway system; steam locomotives were expensive to build and needed lots of labour-intensive maintenance just to keep them running. The trials with the prototype locomotives already mentioned, together with some multiple units built in the 1950s, convinced British Railways that diesels were the way forward. To help them decide the best types of locomotives to mass-produce, a pilot scheme took place in which a number of different manufacturers were approached to build small batches with different engine power ratings, as follows:

- Type A (later Type 1): 800hp–1000hp

- Type B (later Type 2): 1000hp–1250hp

- Type C (later Type 4): 2000hp and over.

Type A

The most successful Type A/Type 1 design was the English Electric Type 1 (nowadays known as the Class 20), among the first to be delivered from 1957 onwards, which had an engine rated at 1000hp and followed common steam locomotive practice, having a cab at only one end and a long bonnet, which housed the engine and generator, in place of the boiler. Several examples are still in use today.

Type B

The Type B locomotives were conceived for light passenger and goods work. Most were early casualties of the Beeching closures; as goods yards and branch lines closed, the purpose for the Type B designs disappeared. The most successful, and longest-lived, class was that developed by Brush, and delivered from

Wheel arrangement	UIC Classification	Notes	British locomotives using the arrangement
O-O O-O	B-B	The axles of each bogie are linked by drive shafts	'Warship' diesel hydraulics on the Western Region
OO OO	Bo-Bo	Each axle is individually driven by a traction motor	English Electric Type 1 (Class 20), Sulzer Type 2 (Class 25)
OOO OOO	A1A-A1A	The outer axles on each bogie are driven, with the middle ones unpowered	Brush Type 2 (Class 30 & 31)
OOO OO	Co-Bo	Each axle is individually driven by a traction motor	Metropolitan Vickers Type 2 Pilotscheme locomotives only
O-O-O O-O-O	C-C	The axles of each bogie are linked by drive shafts	'Western' diesel hydraulics on the Western Region
OOO OOO	Co-Co		LMS 10000, English Electric Type 3 (Class 37), Brush/Sulzer Type 4 (Class 47)
oOOO OOOo	1Co-Co1	The outer axle on each bogie is unpowered; the others each have a traction motor	Southern Region prototypes, English Electric Type 4 (Class 40), Sulzer Type 4 (Classes 44, 45 & 46)

1957–1962. Now known as the Class 31, it has an A1A-A1A wheel arrangement, and a handful are still in use on the main line on test trains. However, they weren't always successful, as the original Mirrlees engines were very unreliable. Once re-engined with English Electric powerplants they were much improved and outlasted other designs by more than 20 years.

Type C

The first Type C designs were all very heavy, necessitating a 1Co-Co1 wheel arrangement. First to be delivered was D200, built by English Electric, in 1958 and it was followed by another nine identical machines. All had a solid and dependable 2000hp engine fitted; they were an immediate success and the class (becoming Class 40 in the 1970s) eventually numbered 200 examples, with the last one not being withdrawn until 1988.

In 1959, the Brush/Sulzer locomotives began to appear, though these were more powerful as they had 2,300hp engines. Again, 10 locomotives were originally delivered from the 'Pilot Scheme' batch and these later became Class 44. Again, success meant the design was perpetuated; 183 more were supplied, though with more powerful 2,500hp engines.

Lessons learned from the pilot scheme diesels

By the early 1960s, enough experience had been gained from the Pilot Scheme batches to enable British Railways to place large orders for whole classes of diesel locomotives. The power classes were redefined as follows:

- Type 1: 1,000hp and under
- Type 2: 1,001hp–1,499hp
- Type 3: 1,500hp–1,999hp
- Type 4: 2,000hp–2,999hp
- Type 5: 3,000hp and over

As can be seen, a need had been identified for power classes in addition to those originally thought necessary, as it was realised that more powerful locomotives would be needed to speed up train services and compete with buses using the new motorways. From the next designs of locomotives ordered, the ones that were most successful and which we still see in use today, are the English Electric Type 3 (now Class 37), introduced in 1960, and the Brush Type 4 (now Class 47), which emerged in 1962 with over 500 eventually being built.

Pocket Fact 🚂

Until recently, the only Type 5 design was the English Electric Deltic, developing 3,300hp. A single prototype emerged in 1955, and was so successful in trials that an order was placed for several examples for the East Coast Main Line (see below).

ⅲⅲⅲ PRESERVED PROTOTYPE ⅲⅲⅲ DIESELS

DELTIC

Number and name: *Deltic*

Class: Prototype

Wheel arrangement: Co-Co

Engine(s): 2 x Napier Deltic, 18 Cylinder 36 piston developing 3,300hp

Transmission: Electric

Builder: English Electric

Used on: British Railways London Midland region and Eastern region

Year introduced: 1955

History: *Deltic* was unlike any diesel locomotive that had been seen before when it emerged from English Electric's West Works in Preston, Lancashire in 1955. It used two lightweight Napier

Deltic engines to give it a huge amount of power and a top speed in excess of 100mph (160km/h). It was finished in a light blue colour scheme with pale cream 'speed whiskers' on the two nose ends, and was very successful in traffic. English Electric developed the locomotive at their own cost in the hope of winning orders to build more, and while none were ordered for the London Midland region, the Eastern Region later ordered a class of 22 of similar design. *Deltic* was later preserved in the National Collection.

Where can I see it?: *Deltic* is usually on static display at one of the National Railway Museum sites at York or Locomotion, Shildon. One of the preserved production machines, 55022 *Royal Scots Grey*, is main line certified and regularly appears on special charters around the country.

D200

Number and name: D200

Class: Class 40

Wheel arrangement: 1Co-Co1

Engine(s): 1 x English Electric 16SVT 16 cylinder, developing 2000hp

Transmission: Electric

Builder: English Electric

Used on: British Railways London Midland region and Eastern region

Year introduced: 1958

History: D200 was the first of the main line 'Pilot Scheme' locomotives to be delivered. Weighing in at a whopping 133 tons, a pair of carrying wheels had to be added at the outer end of each bogie to distribute the load and avoid damaging the track. The class' top speed of 90mph (140km/h) was comparable to the best steam locomotives of the day, and the 200 examples of the type enjoyed a long service life with the last one withdrawn in 1988.

Where can I see it?: D200 is usually on static display at the National Railway Museum at York, and is restored to original condition. Another member of the class, 40145, is based on the East Lancashire Railway and is often used on main line charters as well.

AFTER THE END OF STEAM

Diesel locomotives continued to be built in the 1970s and 1980s, though these were all designed to haul heavy freight trains. The Class 56s and 58s were both Co-Co designs and all were withdrawn in the first decade of the new millennium. The Class 60, introduced in 1989–1990, was the last diesel locomotive to be built in Britain for use on British Rail, and around 20 examples of the class are still in traffic. The Class 66 locomotives that provide the mainstay of motive power for today's locomotive-hauled trains were all built by General Motors in America, with the smaller Class 67s built in Spain but using General Motors engines.

Diesel multiple units were built in vast numbers, using bus engines and semi-automatic gearboxes (again like those used in buses) mounted under the floors, making the entire floor area available for passenger and crew accommodation. Those described as 'first generation' units were built between the early 1950s and the late 1960s, with the last disappearing from the national network in 2003. By this time, the youngest set in service was an incredible 47 years old. They were replaced by similar trains of the 'Sprinter' and 'Pacer' class (the latter with only four wheels per car and bus-type bodies), which use hydraulic transmission.

MODERN DIESEL PASSENGER TRAINS

The revolution in modern passenger travel began in 1976 with the introduction of the InterCity 125 or High Speed Train (HST). These used a single-ended diesel electric locomotive, described as a power car, permanently coupled at either end of a fixed set of coaches to form a multiple unit (so the coaches are called 'cars'). The two power cars each contain a driving cab and a large engine and generator, and the two units provide a total of 4,500hp which is enough to enable the trains to reach a top speed of 148mph (238km/h), though this is restricted to 125mph (201km/h) in regular use. These replaced the 'Deltics' on the East Coast Main Line in the early 1980s and are still in use on many areas of the network at the time of writing.

Since 2000, the use of small but powerful diesel engines has seen some high speed diesel multiple units materialise that have their diesel engines, electricity generators and motors entirely under the floor. Like the HST sets before them, the Voyager class are capable of 125mph but despite being half the length of an HST, with two sets coupled together they can carry 20 percent more passengers.

Monorails

The first monorail was introduced in Russia in 1820, and the first one in the UK was patented just a year later. In the beginning, most traffic took the form of hand-propelled wagons for the moving of goods. In 1888, the Listowel & Balybunion Railway in Ireland was the first monorail to use locomotives; it used an unusual 0-3-0T with two boilers, one either side of the raised single rail, to haul passenger and goods trains. Modern monorails use electric traction, and trains usually take the form of multiple units. The Tokyo Monorail, introduced in the 1960s, carries 127,000 passengers each day. Monorails exist in Britain at Alton Towers and Blackpool Pleasure Beach, among other locations.

ELECTRIFICATION: THE WAY FORWARD

THE FIRST MAIN LINE SCHEMES

Even during the 1930s it was realised that electrification was the best way of improving reliability and speeding up train services.

Back then, a low-voltage DC system (that is, with a positive supply and negative return, just like a car battery), using wires suspended from overhead catenary, was the best method available. The biggest scheme to be designed was the Manchester to Sheffield and Wath-upon-Dearne, primarily for the movement of heavy coal trains. Unfortunately, the Second World War delayed progress on the scheme, though a prototype locomotive was built.

THE COST OF ELECTRIFICATION

Electrification is time-consuming and expensive to implement. The famous Woodhead tunnels were old, in poor condition and too small to take the necessary wiring and other structures for the electrification, so a brand new 3-mile long tunnel had to be cut. The electrified line finally opened throughout in 1954, but within a very few years the technology, and in particular the locomotives, looked very outdated.

Just five years after the line to Sheffield and Wath was opened, the first part of the West Coast Main Line was electrified. The new system used a high voltage system at 25kV, and alternating current (AC, like that supplied to your home); this had the advantage that a lighter contact wire could be used, making the support structures less substantial and therefore cheaper. The substations that provided the electricity supply could also be further apart. The disadvantage in the early years of use was that speed control of AC motors was not possible, so the current had to be rectified (that is, converted to DC before it could be used, meaning that a mercury arc rectifier (see p.170) had to be carried in the locomotive. More recently, technology was developed that allows the control of AC motors, making the electric locomotive even more versatile and lighter.

THE CHANGING FACE OF THE WEST COAST MAIN LINE

Electric locomotives were used on all long-distance express passenger trains from 1959 until 2001. Similar to the 'Pilot Scheme' diesels, the original 100 electric locomotives for the West Coast

Main Line were spread between Classes AL1–AL5 (later Classes 81 to 85), with each class a different type supplied by a different manufacturer. When the West Coast electrification expanded, 100 more locomotives to Class 86 were built from 1965. This time the locomotives were all identical but the building of them was split between British Rail's own workshops and those of English Electric. Some of this type are still in traffic. In the 1970s, when the electrification finally reached Glasgow, the 36 Class 87s were introduced; these have now all been withdrawn. To modernise the fleet in the late 1980s and replace the ageing Classes 81–85, the Class 90s were introduced. Fifty were built in total, and most are still in service, though many have now moved to East Anglia.

Pocket Fact

The Advanced Passenger Train was British Rail's bold attempt at introducing a 150mph electric service for the London–Glasgow line. It was introduced in 1979 and featured tilting coaches that enabled it to take curves much faster than existing trains. Initially successful, a number of teething problems with the tilt mechanism and suspension became apparent and the project was abandoned in 1986. Part of a set is preserved at Crewe Heritage Centre.

In 2001, Virgin Trains introduced the first of its Class 390 Pendolino units. These operate in nine-car sets and can travel at up to 140mph on some sections of the West Coast Main Line. Like the APT, they have a tilting mechanism that enables them to take sharp curves at high speed; in fact, British Rail sold the APT designs to the company that made the Pendolinos, so the technology has come full circle.

Pendolinos are now in service between London and Glasgow, Liverpool, Manchester and Birmingham. One set was badly damaged in the Tebay rail crash and was replaced for a time with a Class 90 and a set of coaches painted in a similar colour scheme to the Class 390 sets. Enthusiasts dubbed this train the 'Pretendolino'.

THE EAST COAST MAIN LINE

The electrification of the East Coast Main Line was planned in the 1960s, but the work then taking place on the west coast was proving to be more expensive and time consuming than originally thought. While some preliminary work had been done to the East Coast line, such as raising bridge decks where necessary, a cash-strapped BR was forced to postpone the scheme, which didn't resume until 1985 and was finally completed in 1990.

The Channel Tunnel 'Eurostar'

With the opening of the Channel Tunnel in 1994, a new fleet of high speed trains was introduced to carry foot passengers between Britain and mainland Europe.

The trains were designated TGV-TMST, or Class 373, by British Rail, but are commonly called 'Eurostars' after the company that operates them. They are dual voltage units, operating from 25kV AC overhead catenary or 750V DC third rail; though the latter is not normally required since the opening of St Pancras International station and the High Speed 1 rail link. The sets consist of two streamlined power cars, one at each end of the train, with 18 coaches in between them carrying a total of 750 passengers. The length of a full train is just under 400 metres.

UNDERGROUND RAILWAYS

THE LONDON UNDERGROUND

- The first underground railway to open in London was the Metropolitan Railway in 1863.

- The Metropolitan, like the Circle and District lines, isn't a true 'tube' railway, as it was built by digging a cutting and then building a roof over the top – a technique known as 'cut and cover'.

- The first underground railways used steam locomotives, but the smoke was a problem in the long tunnels.

- The first tube railway, the City & South London line, opened in 1890 and used electric traction from the outset. It is now part of the Northern Line's City Branch.

- The London Underground system has some 270 stations and 250 miles of track, and carries about 3 million passengers every day.

Top 10 London Underground stations

1. The busiest station on the underground in terms of passengers per year is Victoria, with 77 million.

2. *The busiest station during the weekday morning rush hour is Waterloo, with 49,000 passengers entering during the three-hour period. This station, together with the adjacent one at Bank, has 23 escalators to handle the crowds – the most on any underground station.*

3. *The deepest station on the London Underground is Hampstead, which is 192 feet (58.5m) below ground level. Correspondingly, it also has the deepest lift shaft at 181 feet.*

4. *The deepest station in Central London is Bank; the platforms aren't used by a 'tube' train but the Docklands Light Railway.*

5. *Baker Street has the most platforms of any underground station, with 10 available for 'tube' and sub-surface trains.*

6. *The underground station furthest from Central London is Amersham on the Metropolitan line, at 27 miles (43km) away. This station is also the highest above sea level, at 482 feet (150m).*

7. *Roding Valley is the least-used station on the underground network, with just 210,000 users each year.*

8. *The first escalator on the underground system was introduced at Earls Court station in 1911.*

9. *Angel tube station has the longest escalator in Western Europe at 197 feet (60m), climbing 90 feet (27.5m) with 318 steps.*
10. *The three smallest stations, each with only one platform, are Heathrow Terminal 4, Chesham and Mill Hill East.*

THE PARIS METRO

● The Paris Metro opened in 1900, and its stations are mostly influenced by the Art Nouveau style.

● The system is the second busiest underground in the world (Moscow is the busiest), carrying 4.5 million passengers every day.

● There are 16 lines covering a total distance of 133 miles (214km) and a total of 300 stations.

● The network was so busy in the 1960s that it reached saturation point, and despite new trains the congestion continued.

● The RER, translating to Regional Express Network, was built from the 1960s and has kept expanding in recent years in order to relieve pressure on the original system. This has added a further 47.5 miles (76.5km) of underground railway to Paris, together with some additional 310 miles (500km) of surface lines.

THE NEW YORK CITY SUBWAY

● The first part of the system opened in 1904, using the same 'cut and cover' method as London's Metropolitan Railway.

● It carries 4 million passengers on average each day.

● There are 468 stations situated on 209 miles of routes.

● Unlike the London and Paris systems, it operates 24 hours a day, 365 days a year.

Magnetic Levitation (Maglev) Trains

The first magnetic levitation system (Maglev) was introduced in Birmingham in 1985. It was just 600 metres long and linked Birmingham International railway station with the adjacent airport; it was closed in 1995 (due to problems with the electronic systems and high maintenance costs) and dismantled. Maglev uses a system of magnets to lift, steer and propel a vehicle along. As such, it is not a railway as there is no physical contact between the train and the guiding magnets. The 'trains' are fast (a Maglev car reached 361mph (581km/h) in Japan in 2003), smooth and quiet due to the lack of friction or moving parts. The large number of powerful magnets needed make the systems very expensive to construct, and reliability can be difficult to achieve in practice; as such the idea has yet to catch on although examples are in use in China and Japan.

3

RAILWAY ROLES

At the height of their popularity, the railways required a vast number of staff to ensure that everything ran smoothly, from the movement of passengers and goods to the maintenance of track and the building of locomotives, carriages and wagons. These days, things have changed and the number of staff involved has dwindled significantly but people power is still the driving force behind the railway. This chapter will examine these roles, both past and present, and look at the vital part they played in keeping the railway moving.

⊞⊞⊞ LOOKING AFTER THE ⊞⊞⊞ PASSENGERS

AT THE STATION

Unless you live near a big main line station, it's quite likely that you can arrive at the station, buy a ticket, board a train and even complete your journey without seeing a member of staff, but just a few years ago even small stations would be a hive of activity.

The station master

The station master was responsible for the running of a staffed station, and usually had a complement of staff under his jurisdiction. The job could be a complex one, and even at small remote stations, like that at Bassenthwaite Lake in the wilds of the Lake District, the post would be well paid and often come with a house close to the station. As such, the station master would have a high standing in the local community.

Some large stations, such as that at Preston in Lancashire, were run by more than one railway company and had two station masters controlling different parts of the station.

Pocket Fact

The station master's role was, until very recently, fulfilled only by men; hence the use of 'master' in the title. The fact that many women are successfully running modern-day stations has seen the title now changed to 'station manager' or simply 'team leader'.

The porter

Until quite recently, railway porters were a very necessary part of the station scene. Before the private car became so widely used, motorways were non-existent so the vast majority of long-distance journeys were made by rail. With large amounts of luggage to be transported, including some very heavy trunks, several porters were required at large railway stations to ensure trains weren't delayed by struggling passengers. In the days when stations were larger, porters were also invaluable for checking tickets and making sure passengers got to the correct platform to board their train. The railway porter was altogether more visible than the station master, as he would do most of the manual work around the station. He was expected to be smartly turned out at all times, and was usually supplied with a company uniform. A house was sometimes supplied but it would be a much more humble affair than the one occupied by the station master, and the income from the job would be very little.

Pocket Fact

The railway porter was immortalised in Edith Nesbit's famous work, The Railway Children, in 1905, and though televised three times between 1951 and 1958 it reached a wider audience in the 1970 film. The porter, Perks, was played by Bernard Cribbins in the film, and the busy but poorly paid life is portrayed to good effect in an endearing fashion. 'Be Mr Perks' is a popular attraction on the Keighley & Worth Valley Railway, where the film was shot.

The booking clerk

At many stations, a booking clerk would be in charge of issuing the tickets to passengers. Unlike the porter, he would have few other duties. However, the position required a degree of education as money had to be handled and books balanced. As a result, the clerk was often a boy of 14 or so, just out of school.

The buffet staff

The buffet on a modern station is usually akin to a fast food restaurant, with minimal staff and often a 'self-serve' arrangement for cold food and drinks, but things were very different before stations were 'modernised' in the 1970s. In the earliest days, there were no corridors linking coaches on trains, and no dining cars, so large stations would be equipped with fully-fledged restaurants with a staff of dozens. When a train stopped the cry '20 minutes to dine!' would herald the arrival of hundreds of passengers, all needing to be served quickly so that their journey could continue. Once dining cars were introduced, the importance of these establishments declined. Thanks to the continuing need for passengers to change trains at many stations, the buffets survived into the 1960s, enabling waiting passengers to enjoy hot food and drinks.

Since all station buffets were modernised from the 1970s onwards, most station facilities now only serve pre-packaged snacks and microwaveable food, with drinks served in disposable cups.

Pocket Fact 🎩

The station buffet was made famous in David Lean's 1945 film Brief Encounter, *and much of the plot in Noel Coward's screenplay was centred around Carnforth station in Lancashire (though the tea room used was a recreation installed in Denham studios). The manageress of the buffet, played by Joyce Carey, provides light relief amid the drama surrounding the main characters. The film is still so popular that the buffet has recently been reinstalled in the restored Carnforth station and the 'Brief Encounter Tea Rooms' are a popular attraction.*

ON-TRAIN STAFF

The driver

In steam days, the driver's task was quite involved. He was responsible for the locomotive, ensuring it was in good condition before the start of the journey and keeping all the moving parts oiled before and during the day's duties. It took many years to become a driver of express trains; boys often began as locomotive cleaners straight out of school to start learning the trade. They would then progress 'through the grades' to become a 'passed cleaner' (where they could begin to learn the job of fireman, see below), then fireman, passed fireman (where they could drive under supervision) and driver. There were several grades of driver, and only the best and most experienced got to work in the 'Top Link' and drive the crack expresses such as the *Coronation* and *Royal Scot*.

Pocket Fact 🎩

Thanks to the romance of many childhood stories, a lot of us grew up wanting to be the driver of a steam locomotive, but sadly it may appear that these dreams will come to nothing since the end of steam. However, many steam railways offer a 'Footplate Experience Course' where anyone can spend a day driving a train. Why not take a look at the website for your local preserved railway and see if they provide this? A list of lines, together with a location map, can be found at www.heritagerailways.com.

Driving modern trains is much easier, and drivers initially welcomed the change to diesel and electric traction. It takes much less time to learn to become a driver today; the posts of cleaner, passed cleaner and even fireman are long gone and a trainee can become a driver in a matter of a few months. The preparation time of a diesel or electric train is mere minutes compared to the many hours needed for steam traction.

Pocket Fact 🚂

Train drivers are very rarely seen in films or portrayed on television. The exception is the 1949 Charles Crichton film Train of Events *which portrays the work of a locomotive driver.*

The fireman

The fireman had the most onerous job of the locomotive crew. As well as maintaining the fire and maintaining steam pressure in the boiler, he was responsible for filling up the tender or tanks with water at intervals, keeping the right amount in the boiler to make the steam, and emptying out the fire grate and ashpan at intervals. Becoming a fireman was a major milestone in an engineman's career. It could take five to 10 years of hard work as cleaner and passed cleaner to reach this point, and it was much more than a step on the ladder to becoming a driver.

Pocket Fact 🎫

The job of a fireman is seen to good effect in the 1954 British Transport film entitled The Elizabethan Express. *The film shows the demanding nature of the work, including how water was picked up while travelling at high speed and how crews were changed using the corridor tender. Clips from the film are available on YouTube or at www.screenonline.org.uk.*

With the dawn of the diesel and electric trains, there was no need for a fireman any more. Initially there were fears that the driver might fall asleep with so little to do when compared with driving a steam locomotive, so the fireman became a 'secondman' and continued to accompany the driver. This soon proved to be unnecessary and most trains now just need a driver and guard, with some lines being approved for Driver Only operation to reduce costs.

The guard

The guard on a modern train has little to do other than look after the passengers' needs and check tickets and is normally referred to as a 'conductor', but until very recently he was much more important. From the earliest days right up to the 1980s, the guard was responsible for the safety of the train itself, and the checking of tickets was undertaken by others. As well as the driver, he was expected to know the route of the train, together with the locations of stations and speed restrictions. He would normally be provided with his own accommodation at the rear of the train and could view the line and signals ahead from his brake van (if on a goods train) or compartment (on a passenger train) by the use of special lookout windows or periscopes. If he felt anything was amiss he was able to stop the train, as a brake valve and hand brake were provided for him.

⊞⊞⊞ CONTROLLING ⊞⊞⊞
THE TRAINS

The signalman

The signalman (or 'signaller' nowadays), even today, does more to keep rail passengers safe than any other member of railway staff. The signals (see pp31–33) are the only means of keeping trains a safe distance apart, and correct control of the points or 'turnouts' (see p.158) is essential to move trains from one track to another.

Signal boxes

In the old mechanical signal boxes, points and signals were usually within sight of the signal box's large windows so that the signalmen could check they were working correctly. This meant that there had to be a signal box every few miles along the line, and thousands of signalmen were needed to ensure the safe running of trains.

While there are some of the old signal boxes still around on minor lines, all main lines are now controlled from 'Power Boxes'. Signallers working in these can set entire routes for a train up to 100 miles of track by the press of a button. Power Boxes have very few windows, but the modern detection systems mean that a big illuminated panel in front of the signaller will show the route and the location of the train.

The signalmen used a series of 'bell codes' (beats tapped out on a bell using the electric telegraph) to communicate with each other and send trains along the line. They had to check each train as it went past and record it in a Train Register. In large signal boxes at major stations, with trains passing every few seconds, there could be five or more signalmen working alongside each other, with a number of 'booking lads' to put all the entries in the Train Registers.

Pocket Fact 📖

The signalman in the BBC series Oh, Dr Beeching, *portrayed by Stephen Lewis, spends much of his time on non-railway activities such as giving haircuts, mending bikes and growing vegetables. The occasional appearance of a train is an annoyance to him. While railwaymen in rural areas may have had some side-lines occasionally, the series does this safety-critical role an injustice.*

⸬⸬ MAINTAINING THE TRACK ⸬⸬

Platelayers and gangers

Platelayers were responsible for doing the manual work on the railway line, making sure the ballast was tightly packed under and around the sleepers, and all the bolts were tight and the rails not worn or broken. A team of up to 10 platelayers, under the supervision of a senior man called a ganger, would patrol a given section of line and would be held to account if anything was found lacking. Without their vigilance the track would be rough-riding and unsuitable for high speed trains or even unsafe. When large numbers of platelayers were called up in the Second World War, track maintenance suffered and speed limits were drastically reduced.

Pocket Fact 📖

In the 1953 Ealing comedy film The Titfield Thunderbolt, *Dan Taylor (played by Hugh Griffith) is referred to as a plate-layer, but is actually seen acting as a ganger supervising a team of volunteers maintaining the track. Platelayers are also seen at work in the 1954 British Transport film* The Elizabethan Express.

⊞⊞⊞ DESIGNING THE ROLLING ⊞⊞⊞ STOCK

The locomotives and coaches for each railway company were largely built in their own workshops, a trait begun by the Great Western Railway. The list of all the designers responsible from the dawn of the railways would be too vast to include here, so we will instead consider the pioneers and the names of the 'Big Four'.

THE GREAT WESTERN RAILWAY

Isambard Kingdom Brunel (1806–1859)

Title: Chief Engineer

Period in office: 1833–1859

Notable locomotives: *North Star* 2-2-2, 1838

North Star is recognised as being Brunel's finest locomotive. Most of his others were under-powered, and he soon brought in another engineer to look after the design and specifications of locomotives, diverting his own attention to the design of structures and work on other railways.

Daniel Gooch (1816–1889)

Title: Locomotive Superintendent

Period in office: 1837–1864 (also Chairman of the GWR from 1865–1889)

Notable locomotives: *Fire Fly, Iron Duke*

Gooch was only 20 years old at the time of his appointment as Locomotive Superintendent, but despite this his locomotives were an immediate success and he is widely recognised as being the finest designer of his generation. He was also responsible for choosing the site of the now world-famous Swindon Works.

William Dean (1840–1905)

Title: Chief Locomotive Engineer

Period in office: 1877–1902

Notable locomotives: 'Dean Goods' 2301 class 0-6-0

260 of this design were built from 1883, and proved so reliable and ideal for their purpose that members of the class survived until 1957.

George Jackson Churchward (1857–1933)

Title: Chief Mechanical Engineer (CME)

Period in office: 1902–1921

Notable locomotives: 'City' class including *City of Truro*, the 'Saint' and 'Star' class 4-6-0s

Churchward is also credited with introducing improvements in coach design, including the GWR's first steel-roofed coaches.

Charles Benjamin Collett (1871–1952)

Title: Chief Mechanical Engineer

Period in office: 1922–1941

Notable locomotives: 'Castle' and 'King' classes, widely recognised as the GWR's finest locomotives. Their design was conventional, however, and with the other railways' designs progressing all the time, the GWR were soon left behind technologically.

Pocket Fact

Collett was often criticised for his lack of innovation in design and comparisons were made between the 'King' class and Stanier's 'Princess Coronations' on the LMS, made all the more embarrassing as Stanier was originally a GWR design office employee.

Frederick Hawksworth (1884–1976)

Title: Chief Mechanical Engineer

Period in office: 1941–1947

Notable locomotives: 'County' and 'Modified Hall' 4-6-0s, 15XX class Pannier Tanks

Hawksworth became Chief Mechanical Engineer during the Second World War and lost the post upon Nationalisation, so his chances to introduce new locomotive designs were very limited. Nonetheless, the 'Counties' were recognised as fine locomotives.

THE LONDON MIDLAND & SCOTTISH RAILWAY

Henry Fowler (1870–1938)

Title: Chief Mechanical Engineer

Period in office: 1925–1931 (previously CME of the Midland Railway, 1909–1923)

Notable locomotives: 'Royal Scot' and 'Patriot' class 4-6-0s

Henry Fowler also introduced a large number of locomotives while at the Midland Railway, and these continued to be built by the LMS, including the 'Jinty' 0-6-0Ts and the '4F' 4-6-0s.

William Arthur Stanier (1876–1965)

Title: Chief Mechanical Engineer

Period in office: 1932–1944

Notable locomotives: 'Black 5' 4-6-0s, 'Princess' and 'Duchess' 4-6-2s

Stanier is recognised as being the finest locomotive designer on the LMS, with his 'Princess Coronations' (Duchesses) the most powerful passenger steam locomotives built in the UK.

Pocket Fact 🚂

Stanier is remembered for his express passenger locomotives and 'Black Fives', but he also designed some very successful large tank locomotives. Of the 243 that were built, 37 were a more powerful variant designed for London suburban work. One of the latter, No 2500, has survived and is in the National Railway Museum in York. Stanier also produced a design for a smaller tank locomotive; 139 of these were built, but were unsuccessful and all were scrapped.

Charles Fairburn (1887–1945)

Title: Chief Mechanical Engineer

Period in office: 1944–1945

Notable locomotives: 'Fairburn Tank' class of 2-6-4Ts

Charles Fairburn died of a heart attack just a year after taking up the post of CME, but his only locomotive class is still recognised as being one of the finer LMS tank engines and two are preserved on the Lakeside & Haverthwaite Railway in Cumbria.

Henry George Ivatt (1886–1976)

Title: Chief Mechanical Engineer

Period in office: 1946–1947 (until Nationalisation)

Notable locomotives: 'Mickey Mouse' Class 2 2-6-0s and 2-6-2Ts, 'Flying Pig' Class 4 2-6-0s

Ivatt's designs are recognised as being practical and modern, and even ahead of their time; several of his designs were modified and used as the basis for the BR Standard classes, which continued to be built into the late 1950s.

THE LONDON & NORTH EASTERN RAILWAY

Herbert Nigel Gresley (1876–1941)

Title: Chief Mechanical Engineer

Period in office: 1923–1941 (previously CME of the Great Northern Railway, 1911–1922)

Notable locomotives: 'A1' and 'A3' class, including *Flying Scotsman*, 'A4' class, including *Mallard*, V2 class 2-6-2, including *Green Arrow*

Sir Nigel Gresley, as he was usually known, also introduced some fine tank locomotives and many coaching stock improvements, together with the first of the 'EM1' electric locomotives used on the Manchester, Sheffield and Wath main line.

Edward Thompson (1881–1954)

Title: Chief Mechanical Engineer

Period in office: 1941–1946

Notable locomotives: 'B1' class 4-6-0

Thompson also modified a number of Gresley's locomotives, but the changes made them look hideous and perform poorly, and many of his other designs were unsatisfactory. However, the 'B1s' were fine locomotives that were considered to be on a par with Stanier's 'Black 5s' on the LMS.

Arthur Peppercorn (1889–1951)

Title: Chief Mechanical Engineer

Period in office: 1946–1947 (until Nationalisation)

Notable locomotives: 'A1' and 'A2' class 4-6-2s, including *Blue Peter*

Arthur Peppercorn put many of Thompson's mistakes right in his short career on the LNER. The famous new-build 'A1', 60163 *Tornado*, was constructed to Peppercorn's original design.

THE SOUTHERN RAILWAY

Richard Edward Lloyd Maunsell (1868–1944)

Title: Chief Mechanical Engineer

Period in office: 1923–1937 (previously CME of the South Eastern & Chatham Railway, 1913–1922)

Notable locomotives: 'Lord Nelson' class 4-6-0 and 'Schools' class 4-4-0

Maunsell's 'Schools' class was the last 4-4-0 design to be built in Britain. This wheel arrangement was seen as outdated by the late 1920s and larger locomotives were preferred. However, the Southern Railway had a number of lines with short turntables at their termini so a smaller design was chosen.

Pocket Fact

Maunsell's 'Schools' class was fast and powerful for its size. The fastest speed recorded by the class was an incredible 95mph.

Oliver Vaughan Snell Bulleid (1882–1970)

Title: Chief Mechanical Engineer

Period in office: 1937–1947 (until Nationalisation, continuing on British Railways' Southern Region until 1950)

Notable locomotives: 'Merchant Navy' and 'West Country/ Battle of Britain' class 4-6-2s, Q1 'Coffee Pot' 0-6-0s

Bulleid also introduced many electric multiple units, including the only double-deck train to operate in Britain, and two diesel locomotives. His last project on British Railways was an unusual prototype double-bogie steam locomotive called *Leader* which, sadly, was a failure.

BRITISH RAILWAYS

Robert Arthur 'Robin' Riddles (1892–1983)

Title: Railway Executive Member for Mechanical and Electrical Engineering

Period in office: 1948–1953

Notable locomotives: All BR Standard steam locomotives including 8P 4-6-2 71000 *Duke of Gloucester*, the 'Britannia' class and the 9Fs including *Evening Star*

Riddles retired in 1953 with the abolition of the Railway Executive, but his designs continued to be built until 1960. Shortly after Riddles' retirement British Railways moved over to diesel and electric traction, with design and construction largely by outside companies.

Pocket Fact 🏛

A total of 999 BR standard class locomotives were built, with the last being completed in 1960. When they were designed it was expected that steam would continue into the 1980s but instead most had a life of around 15 years.

4

FAMOUS TRAINS AND THEIR ROUTES

We've looked at the railways in terms of their purpose, as a mover of large volumes of goods and passengers – something the railway was, and still is, very good at. When we think of railways, though, we don't often picture their purpose, instead we conjure up romantic images of the bygone days of restaurant cars, on-train kitchens and at-seat service of the type seen in old black-and-white films.

These trains are fondly remembered by those that travelled on them (or even by those who have only heard of them) but, sadly, these famous trains are now consigned to the history books. Fortunately, there are now a number of main line 'Steam Specials' that run throughout the year that recapture the atmosphere of these special trains.

ⅲ NAMED TRAINS OF ⅲ THE 'BIG FOUR'

In the glamour days of the 1920s and 1930s, the 'Big Four' railway companies (see pp11–12) had a number of prestige trains or flagship services that offered fast timings, good quality dining facilities, and in some cases levels of comfort that bordered on decadence. To give these trains an identity and set them apart from the hundreds of other ordinary services, they were given names that conjured up the image the companies wished to project.

All named trains were suspended for the duration of the Second World War, but many were reinstated afterwards, either by the

'Big Four' companies before 1948 or by British Railways from 1948 onwards.

THE SOUTHERN RAILWAY

The Atlantic Coast Express (the 'ACE')

Type: Holiday express

Year introduced: 1926

Year withdrawn: 1964

Starting point: London Waterloo

Destinations: Padstow (Cornwall), Bude (Cornwall), Exeter (Devon), Ilfracombe (Devon), Plymouth (Devon)

The route: The train used the Southern main line to Exeter via Basingstoke, Salisbury and Templecombe. The train would split at Exeter for the Devon destinations and again at Okehampton for the Cornish seaside towns.

History: The 'ACE' was the Southern Railway's rival to the Great Western Railway's 'Cornish Riviera Express' (see p.100), though it couldn't compete with the GWR train in terms of speed due to the circuitous and steep route beyond Exeter. The 'ACE' was extremely popular, particularly in the height of the summer tourist season and passenger numbers were so high that at times it ran as five separate trains all the way from London. Its popularity declined in the 1960s as more people turned to their private cars for holiday journeys, and the last 'ACE' ran at the end of the 1964 summer season.

Reliving the experience today: The route between Waterloo and Exeter survives as the West of England Main Line, though much of the remainder has now closed, including the branch lines in Devon and Cornwall. First Great Western revived the 'Atlantic Coast Express' name in 2008, though this train bears no relation to its predecessor, using a completely different line and formed of a standard HST set (see p.67). An impression of the 'ACE' on the rural Cornish branches can be had by visiting the

Bodmin & Wenford Railway in Cornwall, which currently operates one of the locomotives that once worked on the nearby Padstow line. Visit www.bodminandwenfordrailway.co.uk for information.

Pocket Fact 🎫

Part of the now-disused route of the 'ACE' featured in episode six of the BBC series James May's Toy Stories, *in which an attempt was made to re-lay the entire 10-mile Barnstaple to Bideford line in model form.*

The Bournemouth Belle

Type: Pullman luxury dining

Year introduced: 1931

Year withdrawn: 1967

Starting point: London Waterloo

Destinations: Bournemouth Central, later Southampton and Bournemouth West

The route: The train travelled through the Surrey and Hampshire countryside, running via Basingstoke and Winchester to Southampton and Bournemouth. Journey time was approximately two hours.

History: The Bournemouth Belle originally began as a summer Sundays-only service, but it proved so popular that it was gradually extended to run on all weekends and summer weekdays, and by 1936 it was a daily working. It was steam-hauled for most of its life, only being diesel-hauled for the final two years before its withdrawal in 1967.

Reliving the experience today: The Pullman train company VSOE (Venice–Simplon Orient Express) operates regular steam specials with full Pullman dining in authentic Pullman cars on a regular basis from London Victoria to a variety of destinations, including Guildford and Bristol. The locomotive used is often 35028 *Clan Line* of the Bulleid 'Merchant Navy' class, which were often used on the original trains. Visit www.orient-express.com for information.

The Brighton Belle

Type: Pullman luxury dining

Year introduced: 1908 (as the steam-hauled 'Southern Belle'), becoming the 'Brighton Belle' in 1934

Year withdrawn: 1972

Starting point: London Victoria

Destinations: Brighton

The route: The train ran on the electrified London–Brighton main line, covering the 51 miles in 60 minutes.

History: The Southern Belle was introduced by the London, Brighton & South Coast railway to provide luxury travel for wealthy city dwellers. To make full use of the electrified main line that stretched between London and Brighton by the early 1930s, three new five-car electric trains were constructed and entered service in 1933. The trains usually worked in pairs to make a 10-car unit, with the third set acting as a spare.

Reliving the experience today: There are no electric Pullman trains at the time of writing, although most of the cars survive and the 5BEL Trust has embarked on a full-scale restoration of a set with the aim of bringing back the Brighton Belle in time for the London 2012 Olympic Games. Visit www.brightonbelle.com for information.

Pocket Fact

The 'Brighton Belle' sets were the first electric all-Pullman trains in the world. They were popular and comfortable and had a long service life, with the service only being withdrawn in 1972 because the stock was worn out and deemed too costly to replace.

The Devon Belle

Type: Pullman luxury dining

Year introduced: 1947

Year withdrawn: 1954

Starting point: London Waterloo

Destinations: Exeter Central, Exeter St David's, Barnstaple, Plymouth (until 1949) and Ilfracombe

The route: The train took a similar route to that of the 'ACE', but travelled non-stop to Sidmouth Junction. A locomotive change would usually take place at Exeter Central where the 12-coach train would be split into two, with four for Plymouth and eight for the steeply graded Ilfracombe branch line.

History: The Devon Belle was introduced by the Southern Railway after the war to encourage the wealthier inhabitants of England to resume their holiday jaunts. Two special observation cars were constructed to give passengers superb views of the stunning scenery on the Ilfracombe line. Unfortunately, with severe shortages still biting after the Second World War, the passenger numbers were much lower than were hoped for. The Plymouth section of the train was not run after 1949, and despite further cutbacks the Devon Belle was deemed a failure and was withdrawn at the end of the 1954 summer season.

Reliving the experience today: The Ilfracombe branch has long since closed, and modern trains do not come close to recreating the experience of the Devon Belle. Fortunately, the two observation cars survive in preservation, one on the Swanage Railway in Dorset and the other on the Dartmouth Steam Railway in Devon. Visit www.swanagerailway.co.uk and www.dartmouthrailriver.co.uk to find out more about these cars and their operation.

SOUTHERN RAILWAY/LONDON MIDLAND & SCOTTISH RAILWAY (JOINT)

The Pines Express

Type: Holiday express

Year introduced: 1927 (as a named train, launched as an unnamed express by the London & North Western Railway and Midland Railway in 1910)

Year withdrawn: 1967

Starting point: Manchester London Road (now Piccadilly)

Destinations: Bournemouth West (extended to Poole 1965–1967)

The route: The train used travelled via Birmingham and Bristol to Bath Green Park and then via the famous Somerset & Dorset Railway via Templecombe to Bournemouth.

History: Unlike many other holiday expresses, the Pines Express was successful enough to run all year round. In later years, portions were run from Sheffield and Liverpool. The train is always remembered for its journey along the highly picturesque Somerset and Dorset railway, though it was re-routed via the former Great Western line through Oxford, Reading and Southampton from 1962. The Somerset and Dorset line closed in 1966 and is much missed by enthusiasts.

Reliving the experience today: With the Somerset and Dorset line gone, there is not currently an opportunity to experience the beauty of the route other than by walking along accessible sections of the disused trackbed. However, the Somerset & Dorset Railway Heritage Trust is actively working to restore sections of the line at Midsomer Norton South station, and the North Dorset Railway Trust has a base at Shillingstone station. A narrow gauge line, the Gartell Light Railway, also runs along a short section of the trackbed near Templecombe. More information can be found at www.sdrt.org and www.shillingstone-station-project.co.uk. A similar 'Steam to the Sea' experience is offerer by the West Somerset Railway (www.west-somerset-railway.co.uk).

Pocket Fact 🚂

Two of the locomotives that were specifically built to work on the Somerset & Dorset Railway have survived. At the time of writing, 53809 is running on the North Yorkshire Moors Railway and 88 is in traffic on the West Somerset Railway.

THE LONDON MIDLAND & SCOTTISH RAILWAY

The Royal Scot

Type: Prestige express

Year introduced: 1862 (by the London and North Western Railway, perpetuated by the LMS and British Railways)

Year withdrawn: 2003

Starting point: London Euston

Destinations: Glasgow Central

The route: The train used the West Coast Main Line via Rugby, Lichfield, Crewe, Preston and Carlisle.

History: The Royal Scot was always a prestige train and was hauled by the best locomotives available. From 1927 the 'Royal Scot' class were used (as might be expected) and by 1937 the 'Princess Coronations' (or 'Duchesses' as they are often called) were used. Up to the Second World War, the use of these larger locomotives enabled a non-stop London–Glasgow run to be made, with a total journey time of seven-and-a-half hours. In BR steam days locomotives would be changed at Carlisle in each direction, but even so the journey time was reduced by 15 minutes; this was done by limiting the train length to eight coaches to save weight. When diesels and electrics were introduced the journey time fell further, to six hours 35 minutes in 1972 and by the time the named train was withdrawn in 2003, the journey time had fallen to five hours. Today's Pendolinos ply the entire 399 miles in around four and a half hours.

Reliving the experience today: The entire West Coast Main Line survives today as the most important railway line in Britain, but the ultra-fast Pendolino trains don't give passengers much chance to enjoy the scenic countryside as they speed along. Fortunately, during the summer there are many special trains run by charter operators that travel along the route between London and Carlisle (and sometimes further). Passengers travel in traditional coaches at a lower speed, and the trains are often hauled by steam locomotives between Crewe and Carlisle. Many of these tours are run by the Railway Touring Company. To find out when these are running visit www.railwaytouring.co.uk.

The Coronation Scot

Type: Streamlined prestige express

Year introduced: 1937

Year withdrawn: 1939

Starting point: London Euston

Destinations: Glasgow Central

The route: The train used the West Coast Main Line via Rugby, Lichfield, Crewe, Preston and Carlisle.

History: The Coronation Scot was the LMS's answer to the LNER's 'Silver Jubilee' and 'Coronation' streamlined trains. The first few 'Princess Coronation' class locomotives were streamlined and painted blue with silver lines to match the coaches used on the train, and the branding was a great success. The trains were only nine coaches long to keep weight down and speeds up, and while successful the trains were discontinued during the Second World War. The streamlining on the locomotives was removed to ease maintenance, and when the war ended the train was never reinstated.

Reliving the experience today: The coaches on the 'Coronation Scot', unlike those on the LNER's streamlined trains, were not specially built; they were just ordinary passenger carriages repainted into the new colour scheme. While none of the original coaches are believed to have survived there are a number of LMS coaches in use on preserved lines, including on the Severn Valley Railway in Kidderminster. See www.svr.co.uk for information.

Pocket Fact 🚂

Unlike the LNER streamlined locomotives, Stanier's Duchesses were never designed with streamlining in mind, and the sleek bodywork made it difficult to get access for maintenance, so it was removed. One of the surviving Stanier 'Princess Coronation' loco-motives, 6229 Duchess of Hamilton *was recently returned to streamlined condition at great expense. While it is not operational, it can be seen on display at the National Railway Museum in York (www.nrm.org.uk).*

THE GREAT WESTERN RAILWAY

The Cambrian Coast Express

Type: Holiday express

Year introduced: 1927 (as a named train)

Year withdrawn: 1991

Starting point: London Paddington

Destinations: Welshpool, Aberystwyth, Pwllheli

The route: The train used the Great Western main line from Paddington to Birmingham Snow Hill, going via the now-closed Wolverhampton Low Level station. Here, the large 'Castle' class locomotives that brought the train from London would be changed for smaller and lighter ones to take the train over the weight-restrict-ed Cambrian line in Wales. The train avoided Shrewsbury, running non-stop to Welshpool and then to Machynlleth, Dovey Junction (where the Pwllheli portion was detached) and Aberystwyth.

History: The Cambrian Coast Express was one of a handful of named trains that survived the Beeching axe, which saw the culling of most similar services. Operating initially on summer Fridays and Saturdays, the Friday trains were withdrawn before the Second World War. Like all named trains it was suspended during the war, but unlike the Devon Belle it became very popular when it was reinstated and ran all week and all year round under British Railways. With the closure of the line to Wolverhampton Low Level its starting point changed to London Euston. Though trains still used the route, the name was withdrawn as the prestige associated with named trains declined.

Reliving the experience today: While the through express trains from Paddington via Birmingham to Pwllheli and Aberystwyth are long gone, a steam-hauled Cambrian Coast Express returned to the Machynlleth–Porthmadog and Pwllheli lines in 2006. This was successful and has been repeated every summer since by West Coast Railways (www.westcoastrailways.co.uk), though the train is now known simply as the 'Cambrian'. West Coast Railways has confirmed that the 'Cambrian' specials will resume in 2012 following a signalling upgrade on the section of line over which it runs.

The Cornish Riviera Express

Type: Long-distance express

Year introduced: 1904

Year withdrawn: Still in operation

Starting point: London Paddington

Destinations: Penzance, Falmouth, Weymouth, Ilfracombe, Minehead and Newquay

The route: The train uses the Great Western main line from Paddington and crosses Brunel's famous Royal Albert Bridge into Cornwall at Saltash.

History: The Cornish Riviera Express was a much faster train than the Southern's 'ACE', and in steam days it managed to avoid stopping to detach coaches at many junctions by using 'slip coaches'. These had a special uncoupling and braking mechanism, enabling the guard in the section being detached to uncouple it from the rest of the train while on the move and bring it to a halt in the right place.

Reliving the experience today: Today's 'Cornish Riviera Express' takes the form of a High Speed Train, but apart from the detachable portions, which are no longer used, the route is the same as that travelled in steam days. The train is operated by First Great Western, and details can be found at www.nationalrail.co.uk.

Pocket Fact 🎫

Until the late 1960s, long distance trains often had full restaurant facilities on board. Restaurant cars had kitchens capable of cooking full three-course meals, and passengers were served at their tables, just as they would in a high-class restaurant. Some of the more prestigious main line steam specials offer this facility today, but tickets cost in the region of £250 per person for the top 'Premier Dining' service.

THE LONDON & NORTH EASTERN RAILWAY

The Flying Scotsman

Type: Prestige express

Year introduced: 1924 (as a named train, originally 1862)

Year withdrawn: Still in operation

Starting point: London King's Cross

Destinations: Edinburgh Waverley

The route: The train uses the East Coast Main Line from London via Peterborough, York and Newcastle to Edinburgh.

History: The *Flying Scotsman* was originally called the 'Special Scotch Express' (though was always given the nickname of its current title). It became a prestige dining train in the late Victorian era, before which time passengers had to dine at York. Even removing this delay, the train journey was slow at eight hours 15 minutes for the 393-mile journey. In 1928, with the A1 class locomotive *Flying Scotsman* itself in charge, and a corridor tender (see p.168) in use to permit crew changes on the move, the first ever non-stop run between the capitals took place with a journey time of seven-and-a-half hours.

Reliving the experience today: The East Coast Main Line survives today as an important route, and its electric trains speed along effortlessly at 125mph (200km/h). However, part of the spirit of the *Flying Scotsman* can be recaptured on one of the many steam specials that run from King's Cross to York, Carlisle and even to Edinburgh. These can no longer be non-stop due to a lack of water facilities on the current network, but are still the best way to enjoy the route. Tours are operated by the Railway Touring Company (see the 'Royal Scot' section on pp97–98) and by Steam Dreams www.steamdreams.co.uk.

Pocket Fact

In the late 1920s, the Flying Scotsman *was a prestige train in every sense of the word. The catering facilities were as good as many top class hotels could deliver, and there was even a barber's shop on board.*

The Silver Jubilee

Type: Luxury streamlined express

Year introduced: 1935

Year withdrawn: 1939

Starting point: London King's Cross

Destinations: Newcastle (later extended to Edinburgh)

The route: When introduced, the train travelled along 260 miles of the East Coast Main Line to Newcastle. The journey was later extended along the full 393-mile route.

History: The Silver Jubilee was the train that started the high-speed streamlining craze in Britain. It was introduced to celebrate the Silver Jubilee of King George V, and was finished in a striking silver livery. Even the coaches were streamlined, and the train was articulated to save weight and give a smoother ride for passengers. High speed was always the ethos of the train. On one of its first runs 112.5mph was reached, a record for the time, and the train originally consisted of only seven coaches to keep weight as low as possible. When it was found that the A4 locomotives used had a reserve of power, an extra coach was added to the formation. The success of the Silver Jubilee was followed by two other streamlined trains, the Coronation and West Riding Limited in 1937. The Coronation train formation ended with a distinctive 'Beavertail' streamlined observation saloon. Two were made, and both survive although they were rebuilt into a more angular style by British Railways. One of the pair is currently being restored to original shape and condition for use on preserved lines. All trains were withdrawn at the outbreak of the Second World War and not reinstated.

Reliving the experience today: Unfortunately, all of the Silver Jubilee vehicles were scrapped, along with the original A4 class locomotives that carried the striking silver and grey livery. Another class member, 60019 *Bittern*, was painted to masquerade as class pioneer 2509 *Silver Link* for a short time but has now returned to the main line in its own guise. Nonetheless, you can still travel behind an A4 from King's Cross to Newcastle (or vice versa) on a small number of steam charters. A list of all those running each year, and the companies that promote them, can be found on www.uksteam.info.

Streamlining

The streamlining craze of the 1930s was more than just a fad; while it made the trains look modern and glamorous there were other benefits. The 'Silver Jubilee' train sets were fully streamlined, so as well as sleek locomotives with aerodynamic fairings, the coaches were fitted with fairings between the bogies to cut wind resistance, and flexible covers were stretched between the coach ends for the same purpose. It all added up to a vast saving on steam, and therefore coal and water, with a streamlined express using 40% less power than a comparable un-streamlined one.

The Master Cutler

Type: Restaurant car express (until 1958); Pullman luxury dining (from 1958 until 1966)

Year introduced: 1947

Year withdrawn: Still in operation (though briefly de-named in the 1980s)

Starting point: Sheffield Victoria (until 1968); Sheffield Midland (1968–1996 and 2008–present); Leeds (1996–2008)

Destinations: London Marylebone (until 1958); London King's Cross (1958–1968 and 1987–1996); London St Pancras (1968–1987 and 1996–present)

The route: When the train was introduced, Sheffield was renowned for its high quality steel for cutlery and tools, hence the train's name. The service ran on the old Great Central Main Line from Sheffield Victoria (now closed) to London Marylebone, but as the route's status declined this was changed to the East Coast Main Line to King's Cross. The name was later applied to a train using the former Midland main line from St Pancras to Sheffield, and the train still uses this route.

History: The Master Cutler has a complicated history, with a significant number of route changes made to reflect changing route status and passenger figures. What started out as one of the highest-profile expresses on the Great Central Main Line became a prestige Pullman train on the East Coast Main Line. Until as recently as 2008, the InterCity 125 version of The Master Cutler carried a Pullman car and a high proportion of first-class accommodation in the formation. Unfortunately, this was changed in December of that year, and the name was given to a standard diesel multiple unit service.

Reliving the experience today: The current East Midlands Trains Class 222 'Meridian' DMUs may carry the name of The Master Cutler but bear no resemblance to the original train, and offer an altogether more modern atmosphere. However, a section of the original route is now part of the preserved Great Central Railway and steam and heritage diesel trains ply the route on many days throughout the year. Visit www.gcrailway.co.uk for more information.

NAMED TRAINS UNDER BRITISH RAILWAYS

While we've already seen that many of the pre-nationalisation named trains were perpetuated under British Railways, a small number of new named services were added to replace those that were lost. Probably the most famous is 'The Elizabethan'.

The Elizabethan

Type: Prestige non-stop express

Year introduced: 1953

Year withdrawn: 1963

Starting point: London King's Cross

Destinations: Edinburgh Waverley

The route: The train used the East Coast Main Line from London via Peterborough, York and Newcastle to Edinburgh.

History: 'The Elizabethan' was British Railways' attempt to revive the pre-war glamour of the 'Coronation' and 'Silver Jubilee' trains, and was launched in celebration of the accession of Queen Elizabeth II to the throne. It lacked the splendour of the 1930s heyday of the fully streamlined trains, and had a high proportion of third-class seats, but was highly popular. It began as a non-stop service, providing a use once more for the A4s' corridor tenders. A stop was introduced for a crew change at Newcastle from 1962 when the 'Deltic' diesels began to haul the train.

Reliving the experience today: A number of main line specials follow part of the route of 'The Elizabethan', and the age of many of the coaches in use on these charter trains are comparable with what would have been used on 'The Elizabethan' in the late 1950s. Two locomotives similar to those used on the original train, A4s

60007 *Sir Nigel Gresley* and 60019 *Bittern* are active on the main line at the time of writing, with 60009 *Union of South Africa* expected to return after major overhaul within a short time. Representing the diesel haulage, 'Deltic' 55022 *Royal Scots Grey* is also used on main line charters. The Great Central Railway in Loughborough offers an 'Elizabethan' luxury dining train service on some operating days; visit www.gcrailway.co.uk for more information.

Pocket Fact 🎗

The Elizabethan features in a 1954 British Transport film enti-tled The Elizabethan Express. *The film depicts the train's non-stop journey, showing the work of the crews, how water was picked up while travelling at high speed and how crews were changed using the corridor tender.*

⊪⊪⊪ BOAT TRAINS ⊪⊪⊪

In the days before mass air travel, private cars and the Channel Tunnel, people wishing to travel abroad caught the train to a port, boarded their liner or ferry, and then got on another train on the continent to reach their destination. Many passengers made do with ordinary service trains and expresses, but for the more afflu-ent traveller the railway companies ran a number of dedicated boat trains to connect with prestige liners.

THE GOLDEN ARROW/FLÈ CHE D'OR

Type: Prestige Pullman boat train

Year introduced: 1926 (in France); 1929 (in England)

Year withdrawn: 1972

Starting point: Paris; London Victoria

Destinations: Calais; Dover (with the outward train running to Folkestone for a period during the 1950s)

The route: The train used the Southern Railway's now-electrified London to Dover main line via Tonbridge and Folkestone, taking 98 minutes for the journey.

History: When introduced by the Southern Railway in England in 1929, the *Golden Arrow* was an all-first class Pullman train normally consisting of 10 heavy Pullman cars and a baggage vehicle. The train connected with a brand new first-class cross-channel ferry, the *Canterbury*. However, in the 1930s as the depression took hold, demand for prestige services fell. Third-class coaches began to be added to the *Golden Arrow* from 1931, and part of the accommodation in the *Canterbury* was declassified at the same time. Suspended for the duration of the Second World War, when the train was re-launched in 1946 the cars were all Pullman once again. Its popularity was such that new Pullman cars were built for the train in 1951 and launched to coincide with the Festival of Britain. Initially the trains were steam-hauled but electric locomotives took over from 1961 when the Kent Coast line to Dover was electrified.

Reliving the experience today: The Bluebell Railway in Sussex regularly runs its own version of the *Golden Arrow* in the form of a steam-hauled Pullman dining train. Visit www.bluebell-railway.co.uk for more information.

THE NIGHT FERRY

Type: Prestige International sleeper train

Year introduced: 1936

Year withdrawn: 1980

Starting point: London Victoria

Destination: Paris

The route: The train travelled via the London to Dover main line, then by ferry to Dunkirk where it was offloaded for its onward journey to Paris.

History: The Night Ferry used first-class sleeping cars specially built by the Compagnie Internationale des Wagons-Lits in France to suit the British rolling stock profile restrictions (referred to as the 'loading gauge'). Five of these sleeping cars, together with two SNCF (French railway) baggage vans were normally used on the trains, with additional ordinary passenger coaches attached to the rear. The first-class coaches and baggage cars were shunted onto special ferries at Dover, and chained to the deck of the ship to stop them rolling around. The ordinary coaches did not cross the channel; these passengers had to walk onto the ferry and get onto another train across the channel. Loading the sleeping cars onto the ferries was time-consuming, and the noise of the securing chains, which stopped the coaches rolling around on deck while at sea, being fastened to their chassis often woke passengers up. When the sleeping cars required renewal in the late 1970s competition from the airlines meant that the construction of new vehicles was not viable and the last Night Ferry was run on 31 October 1980.

Reliving the experience today: The Wagons-Lits cars were all extremely dated when they were withdrawn in 1980, and having had a long and hard working life most were scrapped. One vehicle, 1936-built sleeping car 3792, survives on static display in the National Railway Museum. Visit www.nrm.org.uk for more information.

⠿⠿ THE PRESERVATION ERA ⠿⠿

Since steam ended on British Railways in August 1968, the number of famous named trains dwindled. As passenger numbers fell in the 1970s train travel became altogether less glamorous, and while many trains continued to run on similar routes as previously, rolling stock standards fell, the use of kitchen and restaurant cars was discontinued and named trains were phased out.

When main line steam returned as preservation became more widespread, many steam excursion trains were run as one-offs, carrying the names of long-forgotten, once-famous expresses.

However, there are a small number of recently-introduced named trains that are promising to be just as famous as even the *Flying Scotsman* in years to come.

THE JACOBITE

Type: Steam-hauled tourist train

Year introduced: 1984

Year withdrawn: Still in operation

Starting point: Fort William

Destinations: Mallaig

The route: The train uses the West Highland line between Fort William and Mallaig, via Banavie and Glenfinnan. The return trip is 84 miles long.

History: *The Jacobite* began life as the *West Highlander*, and was actually introduced by the modernised British Rail. It was later renamed the *Lochaber*, and finally *The Jacobite* (after the Jacobite supporters of the exiled King James II with whom the West Highland area has strong links) after it was taken over by West Coast Railways upon privatisation in 1995.

Reliving the experience today: *The Jacobite* runs on weekdays and some weekends throughout the summer season. Visit www.westcoastrailways.co.uk for more information.

Pocket Fact 🚂

The Jacobite *follows in the footsteps of the 'Hogwarts Express', as the viaduct seen being crossed in the movies is at Glenfinnan on the West Highland line. Some of the coaches used on* The Jacobite *are the same ones used on the Hogwarts Express in the Harry Potter movies.*

Other steam-hauled railtours names appear regularly; some are quite newly established while others have been running on and off almost as long as *The Jacobite* has. These include:

- The Scarborough Spa Express
- The Cumbrian Mountain Express
- The Cathedrals Express (running over a number of different routes)
- The Scarborough Flyer
- The Torbay Express
- The Fellsman
- The Waverley
- The Great Britain
- The Dorset Coast Express

Full listings of all trains running each year are available on www.uksteam.info, where information is regularly updated.

FAMOUS TRAINS OF THE WORLD

While you may not have been familiar with all the named trains referred to in this chapter, there are a number of prestige trains, or in some cases their routes, that you're certain to have heard of.

THE ORIENT EXPRESS

Type: Long-distance prestige passenger train

Year introduced: 1883

Year withdrawn: 2009

Starting point: Paris (original route)

Destinations: Istanbul (most frequent route)

The route: The route of the Orient Express has changed many times throughout its history, but the first trains ran from Paris (Gare de l'Est) to Giurgiu, Romania, via Munich and Vienna. Passengers were then ferried across the River Danube to continue their journey, boarding the train at Ruse in Bulgaria and travelling as far as Varna, then travelling to Istanbul by ferry. Later, a new route was added alongside the original one, which allowed the entire journey to be accomplished by rail travelling via the Simplon tunnel, Milan, Venice and Trieste to Istanbul. This became known as the Simplon Orient Express.

History: The Orient Express is featured in many films and books, including the famous Agatha Christie murder mystery, but it also features in Bram Stoker's *Dracula* as the vampire slayer's means of travel to Varna. The Orient Express was most popular between the wars, with three separate routes running; alongside the Orient Express and Simplon Orient Express to Istanbul, the Arlberg Orient Express was added, running to Budapest and Venice via Zurich and Innsbruck. It has a reputation for glamour and prestige and is undoubtedly the most talked-about train in the world.

Reliving the experience today: The Orient Express is no longer in operation, but the private and separate company Venice-Simplon Orient Express runs a number of special trips, aimed at the leisure market, during the summer months. A variety of routes is offered; visit www.orient-express.com for details.

Pocket Fact 🚂

Following on from the most famous work to feature the train, Agatha Christie's Murder on the Orient Express, *a documentary called* David Suchet on the Orient Express *features the popular Poirot actor travelling from London to Prague on the famous train. The story of the route and incidents that led to the writing of the book are discussed in detail. At the time of writing the programme is not available on DVD but is regularly repeated on television.*

THE GOLDEN EAGLE (TRANS SIBERIAN EXPRESS)

Type: Long-distance prestige passenger train

Year introduced: 2007

Year withdrawn: Still in use

Starting point: Moscow

Destinations: Vladivostok

The route: The Golden Eagle travels for an incredible 6,600 miles (10,600km) including along the full length of the Trans Siberian Railroad, via Yekaterinburg, Irkutsk, Lake Baikal, Mongolia and the Russian Far East.

History: The Trans Siberian Railroad is laid to a wider gauge than that used in Britain, at 4 feet 11½ inches (1,520mm). It crosses a record seven time zones, though the Golden Eagle itself crosses an eighth, making it the longest luxury train journey in the world. While service trains take eight days, passengers travelling on the Golden Eagle will spend 13 nights on board.

Reliving the experience today: The Golden Eagle runs on several dates each year from May to September, and still uses the route detailed above. Due to the length of the journey, ticket prices are considerable, with the cheapest being more than £5,500 per person at the time of writing. Information can be found at www.exeterinternational.co.uk.

CALIFORNIA ZEPHYR

Type: Long-distance passenger train

Year introduced: 1949

Year withdrawn: Discontinued 1970–1983. Still in use, albeit using a slightly different route and different rolling stock.

Starting point: Chicago, Illinois, USA

Destinations: Emeryville, California

The route: The California Zephyr runs for 2,438 miles (3,924 km) between Chicago and Emeryville, crossing the Great Plains and the Mississippi River into Iowa. Travelling via Burlington it then runs to Denver and uses the Union Pacific route over the Rocky Mountains, then via the Moffat Tunnel to follow the Colorado River via the Glenwood and Ruby canyons. Cresting the Wasatch Mountains at Soldier Summit, the train then passes into Utah, calling at Salt Lake City before passing into Nevada and following the Humboldt River before crossing the Sierra Nevada mountain range via the Donner Pass and running into California.

History: The California Zephyr's journey is one of the longest and most scenic operated by Amtrak, the current operating company. The route takes the train across seven states: Illinois, Iowa, Nebraska, Colorado, Utah, Nevada and California. The original train took 2½ days to complete the journey, and to enable passengers to make the most of the dramatic scenery the train was timed so that it passed through the most scenic sections in daylight, and several of the cars were fitted with glazed observation domes on their roofs.

Reliving the experience today: Today's Amtrak service uses modern stock and part of the route is slightly different; though the original route survives it is now used solely for freight. Nonetheless, the journey is still enjoyable and the scenery is just as dramatic. Visit www.amtrak.com for more information.

Pocket Fact 🚂

If you long for the nostalgia of the original Budd-built rolling stock, several of the cars survive and some of them can be found at the Western Pacific Railroad Museum in Portola, California. Visit www.wplives.org to see what the museum has to offer.

﷽ NAMED FREIGHT TRAINS ﷽

It wasn't just prestige passenger trains that carried names; some of the best and fastest freight trains were also named in order to encourage companies to send their goods by rail.

THE CONDOR

Type: Overnight freight train

Year introduced: 1959

Year withdrawn: Replaced by Freightliner in 1967. Freightliner container trains are still in operation nationwide.

Starting poin: Hendon, London

Destinations: Gushetfaulds, Glasgow

The route: The train travelled via Leicester and Sheffield and then onto the Settle–Carlisle line, then joining the West Coast Main Line to Glasgow.

History: The name 'Condor' was coined from an abbreviation of the train's use – CONtainer DOor to dooR. It provided next day delivery of the goods it carried. In its early days it was hauled by the unique Metropolitan Vickers Co-Bo locomotives, though these were quickly withdrawn as they were unreliable and replaced with other motive power. At its inception, the train held the record the longest non-stop run for a single crew, travelling continuously for 301 miles between Hendon and Carlisle. The total journey length was 403 miles and the train travelled at an average speed of 40mph, which was incredibly fast when compared with other freight trains of the day.

Pocket Fact 🎫

At its introduction, the Condor was hauled by pairs of Metropolitan Vickers Type 2 (Co-Bo) pilot scheme locomotives; however these were very unreliable and all were withdrawn after a very short life.

One member of the class, D5705, survived into preservation thanks to being used by the Derby rail research laboratory. It is now being restored at the East Lancashire Railway, and details on this unique class can be found at www.d5705.org.uk.

5

FAMOUS RAILWAY STATIONS

From the earliest days of the railways, many stations were built to be imposing, stylish and inviting places, among the finest buildings in the cities and towns they served. Platforms and lines were often covered by large glazed overall roofs, leading to these stations being dubbed 'Cathedrals of Steam'. The best stations are famous throughout the world.

⊞⊞ LARGE STATIONS ⊞⊞

Many large stations were usually constructed in a grand fashion to reflect the importance of their status and encourage trade; however, many were 'modernised' in the 1960s and 1970s, with fine Victorian architecture swept away in favour of Modernist concrete structures. Here are some of the best known large stations.

LONDON ST PANCRAS (NOW ST PANCRAS INTERNATIONAL)

Railway of origin: Midland Railway

Year opened: 1868

Designed by: William Henry Barlow (train shed). George Gilbert Scott (station frontage, the Midland Hotel, which was reopened in May 2011 after a £100 million restoration)

Number of platforms: 15

Number of passengers per year: 20 million

Destinations served: Domestic: Sheffield, Nottingham, Corby, Dover, Brighton. International: Paris, Brussels

Types of trains running: Trains calling at St Pancras include Eurostars to Paris, High Speed Trains (InterCity 125 units) and Class 222 'Meridian' units on the Midland main line and Class 319 and 377 'Electrostars' on the Thameslink services.

Notable features and facts: St Pancras is a Grade I listed building with many notable features. When it opened, the train shed (overall glass roof) was the largest single span structure in the world. The station was threatened with demolition in the 1960s but was saved by a public campaign led by Sir John Betjeman, who later became Poet Laureate. The station was renovated at the beginning of the new millennium, and when it reopened Sir John Betjeman's role in its salvation was celebrated by the unveiling of a statue of him. The International station at St Pancras opened in November 2007; it extends a considerable distance beneath Barlow's great glass roof, which has been refurbished, and is now appreciated by more international passengers than ever before.

Pocket Fact 🚂

St Pancras station and the tunnels nearby featured significantly in the 1955 Ealing comedy film The Ladykillers, *starring Peter Sellers, Alec Guinness and Herbert Lom.*

LONDON KING'S CROSS

Railway of origin: Great Northern Railway

Year opened: 1852

Designed by: George Turnbull, Lewis Cubitt

Number of platforms: 12

Number of passengers per year: 25 million

Destinations served: Edinburgh, Leeds, Newcastle, Cambridge, Kings Lynn

Types of trains running: Trains calling at King's Cross include InterCity 225 sets (Class 91 locomotives, BR Mark 4 coaches and driving trailers), Grand Central High Speed Trains and a variety of diesel and electric multiple units on commuter services.

Notable features and facts: King's Cross station stands on the site of a former fever and smallpox hospital, and platforms 8–10 are also reputedly located where Queen Boudicca's last battle took place. Rumours abound that her ghost haunts a number of passages under the station. The wooden escalators at King's Cross underground station were the site of a disastrous fire in 1987, in which 31 people died. The aftermath of the fire had far-reaching consequences – smoking was banned on the whole of the London Underground, and all wooden escalators have now been replaced.

Pocket Fact 🎩

King's Cross is the location for 'Platform 9¾' in the Harry Potter series. For the filming, platforms 4 and 5 are renumbered 9 and 10, as the real platforms 9 and 10 have four tracks between them. There is a 'Platform 9¾' sign adjacent to the real platforms 9 and 10, and the queues of fans having their photos taken beneath it regularly cause congestion in the station.

LONDON WATERLOO

Railway of origin: London & South Western Railway

Year opened: 1848 (original station); 1910–1922 (present station)

Designed by: William Tite (original station)

Number of platforms: 19 (was 24 from 1994 to 2007 when Waterloo International was in use)

Number of passengers per year: 87 million

Destinations served: Portsmouth, Bournemouth, Southampton, Guildford and many other destinations in the south and south-west

Types of trains running: Trains using Waterloo are mostly commuter EMUs including Class 450 units, though some of the VSOE steam specials start and finish their journeys there.

Notable features and facts: Waterloo was originally called Waterloo Bridge, and in the late 19th century there were many dilapidated and ramshackle stations next to one another that were all called Waterloo. This caused great confusion among the passengers, leading to the London & South Western Railway finally taking matters in hand from 1899 when widescale demolition and remodelling began. The first parts of the new station opened in 1910 but it took a further 12 years to complete the work, thanks to the intervention of the Great War. The present station is the busiest in Britain in terms of passenger numbers. For many years regular funeral trains ran from an adjacent private station to Brookwood Cemetery, but the station was destroyed by the Luftwaffe during the Second World War.

Pocket Fact 🚂

The concourse of Waterloo station was used in several scenes of the 2007 film The Bourne Ultimatum, *where Matt Damon appeared with British actor Paddy Considine. Many television series have also featured the station, including* Spooks, Waking the Dead *and* Only Fools and Horses.

LONDON VICTORIA

Railway of origin: London, Brighton & South Coast Railway ('Brighton side'); London, Chatham & Dover Railway (became the South Eastern & Chatham Railway from 1899) ('Chatham side')

Year opened: 1860; Brighton side rebuilt in 1908; Chatham side rebuilt in 1906

Designed by: A J Blomfield (South Eastern & Chatham station)

Number of platforms: 19

Number of passengers per year: 71 million

Destinations served: Southampton, Brighton, Portsmouth, Ashford International, Gatwick Airport, Dartford, Ramsgate, Dover

Types of trains running: Trains using Victoria are mostly commuter EMUs including Class 450 units, though some of the VSOE steam specials start and finish their journeys there.

Notable features and facts: The present station at Victoria was originally two separate stations, and was unified by the Southern Railway after the 1923 Grouping. One, usually described by railwaymen as the Chatham-side, was constructed by the South Eastern & Chatham Railway as a rebuild of the original station in 1906, and survives as the current platforms 1–8. The other, opened by the London, Brighton & South Coast Railway is normally known as the Brighton-side and consists of the current platforms 9–12 and 15–19. Platforms 13 and 14 are dedicated to the Gatwick Express.

Pocket Fact 🚂

London Victoria features in Oscar Wilde's 1895 play The Importance of Being Earnest. *The title character (Jack, or 'Ernest') was found in a handbag at the railway station.*

LONDON EUSTON

Railway of origin: London & Birmingham Railway

Year opened: 1837; rebuilt 1961–1968

Designed by: Philip Hardwick (original station). Train shed designed by Charles Fox

Number of platforms: 18

Number of passengers per year: 30 million

Destinations served: Glasgow, Birmingham, Manchester, Liverpool, Northampton. Nightly sleeper train to Aberdeen, Inverness and Fort William.

Types of trains running: Trains using the station include Virgin Pendolinos and Voyagers, with a variety of EMUs on local commuter services to Rugby, Milton Keynes Central and Watford Junction. The Caledonian Sleeper is usually hauled by Class 90 electric locomotives.

Notable features and facts: The original station was a fine example of early Victorian architecture. The entrance from the street was made via the famous 'Doric Arch', which was a 72-foot (22m) high stone-built monumental gateway based on the Propylaeum at the entrance to the Acropolis in Athens. It was supported on four huge fluted stone columns and bore the station's name carved into the top 'arch'. This led passengers into a concourse known as the Great Hall.

British Railways decided that the classical style of the station did not suit its new 'electric age' and demolished it between 1961–1962, erecting a new concrete and glass structure in its place that opened in 1968. The 'Doric Arch' was thrown into the River Thames. However, there has recently been a change of heart that may yet see the arch rescued and reinstated as part of a revamp in the near future.

Pocket Fact

The current station building at Euston was described by Times *journalist Richard Morrison as 'one of the nastiest concrete boxes in London … [its design] gives the impression of having been scribbled on the back of a soiled paper bag by a thuggish android with a grudge against humanity and a vampiric loathing of sunlight.'*

Top 10 busiest stations in Britain

1. *London Waterloo*
2. *London Victoria*
3. *London Bridge*
4. *London Liverpool Street*
5. *Clapham Junction*
6. *London Charing Cross*
7. *London Euston*
8. *London Paddington*
9. *Birmingham New Street*
10. *London King's Cross*

Pocket Fact 🚂

While not the busiest station in terms of overall passenger numbers, Clapham Junction is the busiest interchange in Britain, with around 16 million passengers changing trains there every year.

LONDON PADDINGTON

Railway of origin: Great Western Railway

Year opened: 1838 (temporary station); 1854 (permanent station); enlarged 1906–1915

Designed by: Isambard Kingdom Brunel and Matthew Digby Wyatt

Number of platforms: 14 (main line platforms)

Number of passengers per year: 30 million

Destinations served: Bath, Gloucester, Exeter, Plymouth, Penzance, Swansea, Cardiff, Reading, Oxford, High Wycombe, Heathrow Airport

Types of trains running: Trains using the station include First Great Western High Speed Trains (InterCity 125s), Heathrow Express EMUs, Class 165 and 166 'Turbo' DMUs on local services.

Notable features and facts: Paddington's platforms 1–8 are protected from the elements by a large wrought iron and glass overall roof which was designed by Brunel and is recognised as one of his finest station structures. It is almost 700 feet (210m) long and consists of three separate spans, the two outer ones being around 70 feet (21m) wide and the middle one just over 100 feet (31m). Later, a fourth span was added when the station was enlarged, and this now protects platforms 9–12. Platforms 13 and 14 were originally part of an underground station on the Metropolitan Railway called Paddington Bishop's Road, but are now used by local 'Turbo' DMU services. There are two other platforms alongside the former Bishop's Road station, and these are served by the London Underground Circle and Hammersmith & City line trains. Unlike the numerous other deeper level platforms beneath the station, these are numbered as platforms 15 and 16 as a continuation of the main line station.

Pocket Fact

Paddington station gives its name to the popular children's fictional character Paddington Bear, who was found at the station. A statue of the character is located on the main station concourse.

LONDON LIVERPOOL STREET

Railway of origin: Great Eastern Railway

Year opened: 1874 (opened to traffic); 1875 (fully opened)

Designed by: Edward Wilson

Number of platforms: 18

Number of passengers per year: 52 million

Destinations served: Great Yarmouth, Cambridge, Norwich, Ipswich, Chelmsford, Colchester, Southend, Harwich, Stansted Airport

Types of trains running: Trains using the station include expresses to Norwich hauled by Class 90 electric locomotives (displaced from the Euston–Glasgow West Coast route by Pendolinos), together with local services provided by EMUs (including Class 360 'Desiro' units and Classes 315 and 321) and some cross-country services using Class 170 DMUs.

Notable features and facts: Liverpool Street station stands on the site of the original Bethlem Royal Hospital (more usually known as 'Bedlam'). It was originally intended that through trains would run from the Great Eastern Railway onto the underground Metropolitan Railway at Liverpool Street, and the lines drop in level considerably on the approach to the station. Although the link to the Metropolitan Railway was soon abandoned the steep climb for trains leaving the station remains as a legacy of the original plans. During the Second World War, Liverpool Street was the arrival point for hundreds of Jewish children who arrived in Britain as refugees from Czechoslovakia as part of the *Kindertransport* organised by Sir Nicholas Winton.

Pocket Fact

Liverpool Street station concourse featured in a television advertisement for the telecommunications company T-Mobile, in which 350 people took part in a three-minute dance sequence.

OTHER NOTABLE STATIONS AROUND BRITAIN

MANCHESTER PICCADILLY

Railway of origin: Manchester & Birmingham Railway

Year opened: 1842 (as Store Street). Rebuilt and enlarged in the 1880s as Manchester London Road station. Rebuilt in 1960 for the new electric services and renamed Manchester Piccadilly.

Designed by: Building Design Partnership (current rebuilt station)

Number of platforms: 14 (plus two on the 'Metrolink' tram system)

Number of passengers per year: 22 million

Destinations served: London Euston, Preston, Glasgow, Edinburgh, Manchester, Plymouth, Stockport, Manchester Airport, Buxton, Derby, Sheffield, Bournemouth, Bristol

Types of trains running: Express services are provided by Pendolinos, and Class 220 and 221 'Voyager' units. A variety of DMUs and EMUs are used on local services.

Notable features and facts: The main station at Piccadilly is a terminus, with 12 platforms protected by a large glass-roofed trainshed, which is Grade II listed. Platforms 13–14 are the only platforms for through trains, and these are separate from the main body of the station. Until recently, passengers had to walk the length of the terminal station platforms to gain access to platforms 13–14, but a pair of travelators were installed when the city hosted the 2002 Commonwealth Games.

LIVERPOOL LIME STREET

Railway of origin: Liverpool and Manchester Railway

Year opened: 1836

Designed by: Richard Turner and William Fairburn (train shed)

Number of platforms: 9 (plus one underground)

Number of passengers per year: 12 million

Destinations served: London Euston, Preston, Birmingham New Street, Stalybridge, Manchester (Victoria, Oxford Road and Airport), Blackpool, Huddersfield

Types of trains running: Express services are provided by Pendolinos and Class 220 and 221 'Voyager' units. A variety of DMUs and EMUs are used on local services.

Notable features and facts: When Lime Street was built, trains were hauled up the steep incline from Edge Hill by a rope pulled by a stationary steam engine and the locomotives were left behind at Edge Hill station. Trains returning from Lime Street to Edge Hill ran down the slope by gravity, with the speed of their descent controlled by brakesmen.

> *Pocket Fact* 🚂
>
> *Lime Street was voted one of the worst stations in Britain in 2007, but following significant investment and refurbishment it received the 'Station of the Year' award in 2010.*

YORK

Railway of origin: York and North Midland Railway (old station); North Eastern Railway (current station)

Year opened: 1839 (temporary station); 1841 (old station); 1877 (current station)

Designed by: George Townsend Andrews (old station); Thomas Prosser and William Peachey (current station)

Number of platforms: 11 (originally 13)

Number of passengers per year: 7 million

Destinations served: London (King's Cross and St Pancras), Edinburgh, Glasgow, Aberdeen, Inverness, Grantham, Harrogate, Scarborough, Preston, Leeds, Birmingham, Bristol, Plymouth

Types of trains running: Express services are provided by InterCity 225 sets (formed from Class 91 locomotives, coaching stock and a driving trailer), InterCity 125 High Speed Trains and Class 220 and 221 'Voyager' and Class 222 'Meridian' units. A variety of DMUs are used on local services.

Notable features and facts: The old station at York was a terminus, so trains travelling through in each direction had to reverse there; in steam days this meant either turning or swapping locomotives. The old station was replaced with the present one after just 36 years, but survived as a carriage store for a further 88 years before closing in 1965. It is now in use as council offices. The current station was enlarged in 1909 and partially refurbished in 1938, when the current footbridge was installed. Following damage caused by the Luftwaffe during the Second World War, it received heavy repairs in 1947, and was remodelled again 41 years later when the East Coast Main Line electrification reached the town.

EDINBURGH WAVERLEY

Railway of origin: North British Railway

Year opened: 1869–1874 (current station); rebuilt 1892–1900

Designed by: Blyth and Westland (North Bridge trainshed)

Number of platforms: 18 (was 21)

Number of passengers per year: 19 million

Destinations served: London King's Cross, Haymarket, Newcastle, York, Glasgow, Aberdeen, Inverness, Birmingham, Dunblane, Perth, Carlisle, Manchester Airport

Types of trains running: Express services are provided by InterCity 225 sets (formed from Class 91 locomotives, coaching stock and a driving trailer), InterCity 125 High Speed Trains and Class 220 and 221 'Voyager' units. A variety of DMUs are used on local services.

Notable features and facts: There were originally three stations at Edinburgh Waverley, namely the North British Railway's 1846-built North Bridge station, Edinburgh General (opened by the Edinburgh and Glasgow railway in 1847) and Canal Street (also dating from 1847 and built by the Edinburgh, Leith and Newhaven Railway). All eventually came into North British ownership and were collectively known as Waverley (after the series of novels of the same name by Sir Walter Scott) from 1854.

CARDIFF CENTRAL

Railway of origin: South Wales Railway

Year opened: 1850; rebuilt 1932

Designed by: Great Western Railway (current station)

Number of platforms: 7

Number of passengers per year: 11 million

Destinations served: Maesteg, Ebbw Vale Parkway, Milford Haven, Carmarthen, Swansea, Bridgend, Cheltenham, London Paddington, Weymouth, Portsmouth, Nottingham, Birmingham New Street, Derby, Manchester Piccadilly

Types of trains running: Express services are provided by InterCity 125 High Speed Trains and Class 175 'Coradia' units, with local services provided by a variety of other DMUs.

Notable features and facts: Cardiff Central is the largest and busiest station in Wales, and the tenth busiest outside London. The site on which it stands was regularly flooded until the 1840s, but Brunel arranged for the diversion of the River Taff away from the site, thus allowing the station to be constructed.

BIRMINGHAM NEW STREET

Railway of origin: London & North Western Railway and Midland Railway (joint)

Year opened: 1851 (London and Birmingham Railway temporary terminus); 1885 (new Midland Railway station); 1967 (current station)

Designed by: A E Cowper (original 1851 station; F Stevenson (1885 section); Kenneth J Davies (current station)

Number of platforms: 13 (each worked in two halves, A and B, allowing two trains to call at each platform simultaneously)

Number of passengers per year: 8 million

Destinations served: London Euston, Preston, Glasgow, Edinburgh, Manchester, Plymouth, Coventry, Wolverhampton, Newcastle, Bristol, Nottingham, Leicester, Cardiff, Shrewsbury, Holyhead

Types of trains running: Express services are provided by Pendolinos, InterCity 125 High Speed Trains and Class 220 and 221 'Voyager' units. A variety of DMUs and EMUs are used on local services.

Notable features and facts: When Birmingham New Street station first opened, the train shed protecting the trains, passengers and platforms from the weather was the largest iron and glass roof in the world with a span of 212 feet (65m) and a length of 840 feet (256m).When enlarged by the construction of the adjacent new Midland Railway station, further platforms and a large iron and glass roof were added. The roof was substantially damaged by Luftwaffe bombing raids during the Second World War, but was later repaired. In the 1960s, the station was remodelled, and the light and airy glass roofs were swept away in favour of a low concrete structure, on which were constructed a shopping centre, car park and office block. This has led to its current classification as an underground station, and steam trains are not permitted to pass through it. It is currently one of the three least-popular stations in Britain in terms of customer satisfaction.

GLASGOW CENTRAL

Railway of origin: Caledonian Railway

Year opened: 1879; rebuilt 1901–1905

Designed by: Blyth and Cunningham

Number of platforms: 15 (plus two on the Low Level station)

Number of passengers per year: 28 million

Destinations served: London (Euston and King's Cross), Preston, Manchester Airport, Birmingham New Street, Ayr, Stranraer, Kilmarnock, Largs and other destinations in the Midlands, South and South West

Types of trains running: Express services are provided by Pendolinos and Class 220 and 221 'Voyager' units. A variety of DMUs and EMUs are used on local services.

Notable features and facts: Glasgow Central is the busiest railway station in Scotland, and the second busiest outside London. Its most famous feature is the large glass-walled bridge, known to Glaswegians as 'Heilanman's Umbrella' (Highlandman's Umbrella), which takes the station over Argyle Street in the city. It was given this name because it was the location of the original ticket office and also the place where visiting Highlanders would congregate. The structure is very grand, with tall arch-roofed windows.

⨳⨳⨳⨳ QUIRKY STATIONS ⨳⨳⨳⨳

Not all famous stations are large ones. Some stations are famous for other reasons; some are infamous 'blots on the landscape' when innovative design went wrong, while others have quirky features. Here are some of Britain's best quirky stations:

- Llanfairpwllgwyngyllgogerychwyrndrobwllllantysiliogogogoch in Wales has the longest name of any railway station in Britain. Its original name of Llanfairpwll was embellished in the Victorian era to encourage tourism.

- Damems, originally on part of the national network until the Beeching cuts and now on the Keighley & Worth Valley Railway, is Britain's smallest station.

- Corrour station, located on Rannoch Moor on the Glasgow–Fort William section of the West Highland line in Scotland, is the highest main line station in Britain and the most remote, being 10 miles from the nearest road.

- Coombe Junction Halt on the Liskeard–Looe branch line in Cornwall is reputedly the least used station in Britain, with just 42 passengers boarding a train there in the 2009–2010 financial year.

- Beauly, the first station north of Inverness on the Kyle of Lochalsh line, is reputedly the most successful new small station in Scotland. Opened in 2002 (the original station closed in 1960) after a campaign by local residents, the short platform serves a population of just under 1,200, but in 2009–2010 it was the starting point for more than 75,000 journeys.

- Fenchurch Street is the smallest main line terminus in London, with only four platforms and no direct link to the London Underground. Nonetheless more than 15 million passengers a year use the station, compared with fewer than 12 million at Marylebone, the next smallest station with six platform faces.

- The oldest railway station still in use in Britain is Edge Hill in Liverpool, dating from 1836. It has four platforms and around 100,000 passengers a year start or end their journeys there. The oldest surviving railway station, dating from 1830, is Liverpool Road, Manchester, now part of MOSI, the Museum of Science and Industry.

- Bath Green Park (originally named Queen Square until 1954), terminus of the Somerset and Dorset Joint Railway to Bournemouth, had just two platforms but is still recognised as being among the finest buildings in the city and is Grade II listed, still standing almost 50 years after the last passenger train left.

Pocket Fact

The underground station that features in the BBC soap opera EastEnders *does not exist in reality. The building was mocked up outside Elstree Studios in the style of Leslie Green (who designed many underground stations, including Covent Garden) and the scenes are filmed there. The fictitious station is supposedly located on the District Line in the place of Bromley-by-Bow.*

6

A GRICER'S GUIDE

Railways undoubtedly capture the imagination unlike any other form of transport, and many people are fascinated by the different aspects of rail travel. Those who are interested in railways once called themselves 'train spotters', but this term is now seen by many as an insult, mainly thanks to the media using it as a put-down to infer that train spotters are anorak-wearing, decidedly odd people. The preferred term for railway followers in Britain is 'railway enthusiast' – but as that's a bit long-winded they often refer to themselves as 'gricers'.

Pocket Fact

The term 'gricer' has been used to describe the railway enthusiast for many years, and is used both in Britain and America. It is said to date back to the late 1930s and originates from the word 'grouse'; after a successful day's grouse shooting the hunter would come back with a substantial bag of booty. The term 'bag' is similarly used by an enthusiast to describe the recording of a locomotive number in their notebook.

HOW IT ALL BEGAN

Train spotting, or more correctly 'loco-spotting', began as a craze in 1942 thanks to the efforts of the now legendary Ian Allan. Back then, he was a 19-year-old trainee in the Southern Railway's public relations office at Waterloo. He found he was forever answering letters from enthusiasts who wanted information on locomotives, so to save time he suggested putting all the details together in a book that listed all the different types and their details. The PR office wasn't interested, so Allan went on to produce the book himself. *The ABC of Southern Locomotives* proved extremely popular and the first run of 2,000 copies sold out immediately.

Over the next few years, Allan went on to produce similar volumes for the other three railway companies, which proved just as popular. By 1944, he had coined the phrase 'loco-spotting' and it was recognised as a widespread craze when a group of boys were arrested for trespassing on the West Coast Main Line in the Midlands. Allan then formed the Loco-spotters Club in order to encourage the hobby to be undertaken safely. Train spotting (as it was later known when multiple units became more widespread) grew increasingly popular after the war, with interest only beginning to wane with the end of steam in 1968.

THE DECLINE OF THE SPOTTER

Today, with so few types of trains in operation, 'train spotters' as we know them (those who take train numbers from the ends of station platforms) are relatively few in number. Following in the footsteps of the *ABC* guides, a combined volume for spotters and other enthusiasts, *British Railways Locomotives and Coaching Stock* was created and is still published annually. Ian Allan no longer publishes this book, but his business grew from the initial 'Loco-spotters Guides' and his company is now the largest publisher of transport books in the world.

﷼﷼﷼ MODERN-DAY GRICING ﷼﷼﷼

The term 'gricer' no longer applies solely to the dedicated taker of numbers, keen to 'bag' all the operational locomotives and coaches and underline the numbers in his *ABC*. With the death of steam and the loss of the wondrous variety of locomotives that previously existed, the hobby evolved and different facets have appeared. These include:

- Railway photography
- 'Bashing' (see p. 138)
- 'Track bashing' (see p. 143)
- Collecting railwayana (see p. 145)
- Railway group and association membership
- Volunteering on preserved or heritage lines
- Internet forum participation
- 'Armchair' participation through magazines

‖‖‖‖ RAILWAY PHOTOGRAPHY ‖‖‖‖

Railway photography is one of the most popular forms of 'gricing' seen today. When steam specials run on the main line, literally hundreds of photographers (described as 'photters' by the railway enthusiast fraternity) armed with a wide variety of still camera and video equipment can be seen in fields and on bridges along the line. The same scene is repeated at the many preserved railways around Britain and abroad. While it's mostly steam traction that is photographed, heritage diesels and modern trains have their own, admittedly smaller, following.

Pocket Tip

For a list of all main line steam specials running each year, together with approximate timetables, visit www.uksteam.info. Be sure to keep checking the site, as it's regularly updated, in case tours are changed or cancelled at short notice.

Railway photography is a cheap hobby to enjoy once the initial cost of the camera is out of the way. There are so many railways around the country that very few enthusiasts will have to travel for more than an hour to find a suitable location to start snapping away. There is a definite skill and art to getting good train photographs, however, as there are many factors to take into consideration besides the train itself. Using your camera's fully automatic mode will rarely give satisfactory results. A summary of the main points to consider is given below.

Speed of the train

Railway photography is significantly different from capturing a landscape image. Depending on the location, even a steam train may be travelling at up to 75mph (120km/h) and a fast shutter speed (1/500 of a second or faster) will be required to avoid the train appearing blurred. If your camera won't let you set the shutter speed manually, try using sports mode.

Lighting conditions

If light levels are low, for example when low cloud blocks the sun, the train can look very dark in comparison to the landscape around it. In cases like this, it's best to get as close to the train as you can so the train is the main subject. That way, it's less likely to be under-exposed.

When the sun is out, it's best to have it at your back to avoid parts of the train being in shadow when it arrives. It sounds simple, but you need to make sure you are on the correct side of the line when the train appears. Trains can be minutes early or even hours late, and as the sun's position moves during the day your location will need to be carefully planned.

Pocket Tip ▰▰▰▰▰▰▰▶

A useful tool to ensure you choose a location with the sun in the best place for your photographs, the Photographer's Ephemeris, is available on the internet for free at www.photoephemeris.com. It's also available as an App for iPad and iPhone.

Wind

Wind can make or ruin a railway photograph, particularly if taking pictures of steam trains. Always ensure the wind is blowing away from you wherever possible; if it's blowing towards you the smoke from the locomotive can completely obscure the train.

Pocket Tip ▬▬▬▬▬▶

Even a light wind can blow enough smoke to ruin a photograph. If you're not sure of the wind's direction, try holding up a paper handkerchief (or if you don't have one, a long blade of grass will do) and letting it go. The direction it moves as it falls will betray even the lightest of winds.

Gradients

When photographing steam locomotives, the photos always look better if they are working hard, with white smoke billowing upwards to add to the atmosphere of the shot. The best way to ensure you get this effect is to look for a section of railway on which the train will be going uphill. A good map may indicate this, or alternatively you can look for a gradient board at the lineside to help you. Steam locomotives going downhill often have the throttle (known as the regulator) closed, so only minimal smoke (if any) will appear.

Train length

If you want to capture a steam locomotive at work, it often adds balance to the shot if you can take a picture of the whole train. In some cases, the trains can be up to 13 coaches long (including the locomotive, that's around 300 yards or 275 metres!) and to get the whole train in the photograph you'll either need to be some distance away or taking the shot more or less head-on. Alternatively, by choosing the location carefully a long train can be naturally 'cut off' by a tunnel, cutting (see p. 168), copse of trees or a lineside structure such as a station or bridge.

Night photography

Some wonderfully evocative photos can be taken of steam locomotives at night. You'll need the use of a tripod to keep the camera steady, and a long shutter speed (sometimes 30 seconds or more) will be needed to ensure enough light reaches the film or camera sensor to expose the photograph properly. A manual off-camera flash, which can be fired many times while the shutter is open, will add light when it's very dark. This isn't the type of shot that's possible with most pocket compact cameras, but the ghostly effect caused by drifting steam can be very dramatic.

PHOTO CHARTERS

If you're serious about railway photography, a good way to ensure some first-rate pictures is to partake in a specially organised photo charter. These can cost a significant amount of money (between £30–£100 for a day-long event) but that's because a train, and its crew, has been booked specifically for the photographs for an entire day. The train will be run up and down the line repeatedly to ensure all participants get the chance of a great shot, and there will usually be plenty of experienced photographers there to share their experience and give you some useful tips.

⊞⊞⊞ 'BASHING' ⊞⊞⊞

'Basher' is the name given to an enthusiast who follows a particular type of rail traction, and the term is almost exclusively used to describe fans of diesel locomotives. The aim of 'bashing' is to accumulate as much rail mileage as possible behind the diesel class of your choice. Most popular are the classic types, now largely gone from the main line but still appearing from time to time on main line charters in a similar fashion to steam locomotives. Many of the classic types have survived into preservation; enjoying less of a following than steam locomotives, their outings are fewer even on heritage lines, making bashing them even more of a challenge.

TAKING UP BASHING

To become a successful basher it helps to be 'in the know' as to when and where your chosen traction is running. Manoeuvres such as 'drags' (rescuing failed trains) are often arranged at short notice and are not advertised; the best places to find these are on the forums (see p.146). Other special charters are usually organised weeks or months in advance, and the best place to find this information is at www.railtourinfo.co.uk/diesel.html. Heritage lines often hold special diesel events too, so keep an eye on the website of your local or favourite line for details.

To begin you have to select the class or classes you wish to follow, and there's no better way than to make a few journeys behind different locomotives at a diesel gala on your nearest railway. Popular classes include:

Class 20

Nicknamed 'choppers', because of the distinctive exhaust sound, or 'wardrobes', due to the six tall doors on either side of the long bonnet. A small number are still active on the main line on freight duties but they also sometimes appear on passenger 'specials'. A number are also in use on heritage lines. They are instantly recognisable, having a cab at only one end and then a long 'nose' bonnet, akin to the cab and boiler arrangement on a steam locomotive.

Class 37

Given the nickname 'growlers' by enthusiasts due to the engine sound, a number of these locomotives are active on the main line on freight workings and are also sometimes employed on passenger trains. There are around 40 of the class in preservation to date. They can be easily recognised by the bonnet on each end and the use of 6-wheeled bogies.

Class 40

Known as 'whistlers' due to the musical note from the exhaust caused by the turbocharger fitted to the engine. The locomotives were the first express passenger types delivered in the British

Railways Modernisation Plan and have achieved cult status with enthusiasts. The last was withdrawn in 1988, but seven of the class are preserved and one example, 40 145 based on the East Lancashire Railway, is now main line registered and works a number of charters each year. The Class 40 can be identified by the use of a long, angular bonnet 'nose' on each end and a pair of eight-wheel bogies.

Class 44/45/46

These three classes of similar locomotives, all built by British Railways and fitted with Sulzer diesel engines, are invariably treated as one group, nicknamed 'peaks' by enthusiasts due to the first 10 examples (Class 44) being given the names of famous British mountains. There are two Class 44s, 11 Class 45s and three Class 46s in preservation, though none are currently registered for use on the main line. At first glance similar to the Class 40s, the 'Peaks' can be differentiated by the shorter and more rounded nose ends.

Pocket Fact

In 1984 a 'Peak', 46 009, was deliberately and spectacularly destroyed in a televised test to prove the safety of nuclear waste flask containers. A container was fastened across a special 8-mile long test track and the locomotive and an empty train of old coaches sent hurtling towards it at over 90mph. The locomotive disintegrated, its engine being torn out, but the nuclear flask survived unscathed. The video can be found on YouTube (www.youtube.com) by searching for 'Train test crash 1984'.

Class 47

Nicknamed 'duffs' by bashers in their early days, because the class of 512 examples was too common to be worth bashing, their popularity soon grew. While the 'duffs' name stuck, they were also given the more affectionate name 'brushes' after their builder Brush Traction. Followers of the class are thus often referred to as 'brush bashers'. A number are still active on the main line on freight and charter work, while others survive in preservation.

The Class 47 has a distinctive long box shape, with twin cab windscreens on each end and two 6-wheeled bogies.

Class 50

A larger locomotive than the Class 47, the class numbered only 50 examples, thereby endearing them to the bashers almost instantly owing to their rarity value. They were given the nickname 'hoovers' early on due to the sound of the radiator cooling fans being likened to the noise of a vacuum cleaner. The class was withdrawn from British Rail in 1994, though no fewer than 18 locomotives survive in preservation with some registered for main line use. The Class 50s look a little like the Class 47s at first glance, but are longer and have a large headcode box on each end of the roof above the cab.

Class 52

This class was officially known as 'westerns' as they were introduced by British Railways' Western Region and all were given names prefixed by 'Western'. They are also nicknamed 'wizzos' by enthusiasts. They differ from most other diesels by having hydraulic transmission rather than electric motors. They have angular cab ends and unusual 6-wheeled bogies, with only the middle wheels on each axle concealed by frames. They also have cast metal numberplates, a relic dating back to the Great Western steam locomotives they replaced. They were all withdrawn by the end of the 1970s, although seven of the 74 class members have survived into preservation with one registered for main line use.

Class 55

Known as the 'deltics' after their twin Napier powerplants (see pp65–66) of the same name, the Class 55s are probably the most popular of the early diesel classes. Despite the fact they replaced the popular Gresley A3s and A4s on crack expresses they have always had a significant following. They are renowned for their loud exhaust note, which can be heard for many miles around, and the plumes of white smoke produced by the twin two-stroke engines. This, together with the tall bonnet-nosed cab ends and curved double split windscreens make them instantly recognisable.

When introduced in 1961 they were the most powerful production locomotives in the world, developing 3,300hp. They lasted until the end of 1981 when they were replaced by High Speed Train sets. Six of the class are preserved, and at present 55 022 *Royal Scots Grey* is registered for main line use.

Class 57

Introduced from 1997, the Class 57s are known as 'bodysnatchers' to enthusiasts due to the fact they were created by modifying redundant Class 47s with a modern General Motors diesel engine and uprated electrical systems. The initial locomotives were intended for freight trains, but Virgin Trains and First ordered a number of examples for passenger use. The Virgin locomotives have been fitted with different couplings to allow them to rescue failed Pendolino and Voyager units, earning them their nickname 'thunderbirds'. As they share their bodyshell with Class 47s it's often difficult to differentiate between the two types; most class 57s have been fitted with uprated headlamps, but the only sure-fire way to tell is to check the locomotive number. Class 57s all carry their TOPS number, prefixed with the class number, and all are used solely on the main line.

Class 66

The Class 66 is almost as numerous as the Class 47 was at its peak, with 446 locomotives delivered in total. They were all built by General Motors in Canada and shipped to the UK from 1998 onwards, with the last examples delivered in 2008. They are very similar in appearance to the earlier Class 59s (a class of only 15 examples), and earned the nickname 'sheds' due to their angular roofline, which when viewed head-on looks like a garden shed. The class can be seen all over the UK, and the angular cab makes them easy to spot. A bash behind a Class 66 is quite difficult to plan, as they are very rarely used on passenger services.

Class 67

These locomotives are the latest to be built with fast passenger trains in mind, and were introduced from 1999. They were built by Meinfesa in Spain and shipped to the UK, with the last of the class of 30 entering service in 2000. Their top speed of 125mph (200km/h) makes them ideal for rescuing failed trains, and unexpected passenger haulage is a frequent occurrence, particularly on the East Coast Main Line. They are also used on charters and can be found on such wide-ranging duties as rescuing failed steam locomotives and hauling the Royal Train. They can be instantly recognised by their sharply sloping cab windscreen area, which earned them the nickname 'skips' as they were likened to an upturned rubbish skip.

'TRACK BASHING'

Similar to locomotive bashing, 'track bashing' (also known as 'complete riding') is the name given to the enthusiast activity of trying to travel on every section of track in a specific area. This could relate to anything from riding on every heritage railway in a county or every line on the entire national network.

The task may sound easy, if a little time-consuming, but it can be very difficult indeed. For example, if a track basher is trying to ride over every line in their own county, it's not simply a matter of boarding a normal passenger train over every advertised route. Some lines are designated 'freight only' and will not have passenger trains passing along them under normal circumstances. However, once in a blue moon there may be a train diversion due to engineering work or an organised special passenger railtour that will travel that way, and the dedicated track basher will have to keep an eagle eye out for opportunities like this. Again, this sort of information is regularly detailed on the forums.

Railcards

You can keep the cost of track bashing down by purchasing a railcard. These are applicable to people in certain categories:

16–25 Railcard

Previously called the 'Young Person's Railcard', for a one-off charge you can save a third on the cost of standard class tickets for a whole year.

Family & Friends Railcards

Anyone can have one of these; the only stipulation is that you must travel with at least one child. Again, there's an annual charge for the railcard but you can save a third off standard class adult fares and 60% off child fares. Up to four adults and four children can travel on one card.

Senior Railcard

If you're aged 60 or over, you can purchase a Senior Railcard. Similar to the other categories, it has to be renewed annually but you can save a third on the cost of both standard and first class tickets.

Disabled Person's Railcard

If you are registered disabled, you may qualify for a Disabled Person's Railcard. The card covers you and a companion, and will save a third on standard class ticket fares. An annual fee applies.

Network Railcard

If you live around London or in the south-east of England, you'll be able to buy an annual Network Railcard for use on travel around the area. You and three friends can save a third on standard class adult travel, and up to four children travelling with you can also travel for 60% less. Unlike the Friends & Family Railcard, however, one adult travelling alone can also use it.

Full details of all railcards can be found at www.railcard.co.uk.

⊞⊞⊞ COLLECTING RAILWAYANA ⊞⊞⊞

Railwayana is the term used to describe collectable artefacts relating to railways. The articles collected are interesting and varied, ranging from old timetables, tickets and fliers to locomotive parts, old lamps and station benches. They range in value from a few pounds to tens of thousands of pounds, and railwayana is certainly big business. While some items can be found on eBay and other regular online auction sites, because of the value of some items fake goods also turn up on a regular basis and it's very difficult to differentiate between them and the genuine article. For that reason, it's always best to visit a specialist auction to choose at least your first few pieces and to take a look at the vast variety of items offered for sale. An internet search for 'railwayana auction' will bring up results for a number of specialist auction houses and sites, together with a number of other venues that hold occasional railwayana events.

Top 10 types of railwayana collected

1. *Locomotive nameplates (the ornate Great Western brass ones are among the most expensive).*
2. *Wagon numberplates.*
3. *Railway crockery and cutlery.*
4. *Station signs and advertisements.*
5. *Railway posters (the ones from the Art Deco period are the most sought-after).*
6. *Train headboards (such as for the* **Golden Arrow** *and* **Royal Scot***).*
7. *Engine shed plates (each locomotive carried a plate identifying its home shed).*
8. *Railway clocks (either from stations or staff presentation clocks).*
9. *Signalling and signalbox instruments.*
10. *Badges and buttons.*

The list isn't exhaustive and virtually anything to do with railways is collectable.

⸬⸬⸬ RAILWAY MEMBERSHIP ⸬⸬⸬

Wherever you live in the British Isles, you're sure to be within a short distance of a preserved railway. There are over 150 such lines dotted around the country, and almost all of them are run on a charitable basis. They rely on membership fees and donations for their existence and are largely volunteer-run. One of the best ways to participate as an enthusiast is to join a railway association or society. Membership is usually inexpensive, and on the majority of railways it provides many benefits including the issue of regular newsletters and magazines and concessionary travel on some trains.

VOLUNTEERING

Having become a member of a nearby line, you may find you enjoy your visit so much that you want to become involved. The variety of roles that you can join in is vast (aside from the obvious ones of driving or firing the steam locomotives); staff are needed to sell tickets, work in station cafes, look after museum exhibits and, most importantly, restore and maintain the rolling stock. Magazines and newsletters need putting together and distributing, membership needs looking after and events need organisation, and for many tasks you won't need to commit to regular hours or patterns of work. If you pop down to your local line you're bound to find something to interest you, and the atmosphere is sure to be friendly and welcoming.

INTERNET FORUMS

A good way of keeping in touch with the goings-on on the general railway scene is to join an online forum. Two of the major ones are National Preservation (usually called 'NatPres' by its followers), www.railways.national-preservation.com, and RailUK Forums, http://railforums.co.uk, although there are many others. A wealth of information is provided and discussed, and knowledgeable enthusiasts share their experience with others. Real gems of up-to-the-minute information, including unannounced test runs of steam and modern traction and rare passenger haulage (as desired by bashers), regularly turn up on the sites. Another site useful to bashers is www.wnxx.com which regularly details withdrawal of modern locomotives from traffic.

⊞⊞⊞ RAILWAY MAGAZINES ⊞⊞⊞

Whatever your particular passion within railways, you'll be well-catered for in terms of reading material. There's a wide variety of magazines covering the entire spectrum of steam and diesel locomotives, heritage lines and main line specials, not forgetting the nostalgia of days gone by. The titles include:

THE RAILWAY MAGAZINE

The longest-established publication, it's been running for over a century, and covers all things railway from days of old and small preserved steam lines to up-to-the-minute main line transport. With such a wide spectrum covered, many stories are only covered briefly but if you're interested in the general railway scene it's a good source of information.

STEAM RAILWAY

The current market leader in its class, as its name suggests, *Steam Railway* is devoted to all things to do with the steam locomotive. Any goings-on from small narrow-gauge lines to main line specials are reported, and if you want news on your favourite steam locomotive, you are likely to find it here. There are also many pages of good-quality photographs sent in by readers.

HERITAGE RAILWAY

With a similar outlook to *Steam Railway*, *Heritage Railway* also covers a smattering of heritage diesel news.

RAIL

Rail magazine covers the modern image scene but is aimed at rail professionals rather than enthusiasts. While many enthusiasts read it, a beginner can find some of the technical details hard to understand.

RAILWAYS ILLUSTRATED

If you're a heritage or modern diesel or electric fan, *Railways Illustrated* covers many of the news stories, big and small, each month. There's also a small steam section each issue, covering the main news and developments. The paper quality is better than most other publications, giving the photos a much-improved appearance.

RAIL EXPRESS

Similar to *Railways Illustrated* but without the steam content, *Rail Express* deals with today's diesel and electric traction, including up-to-date news and the preservation scene. It also contains a small modelling section.

TRACTION

This magazine is devoted to classic diesels and electric locomotives, with heavy emphasis on the surviving members of the early classes. You'll find information on diesel galas and main line charters together with feature articles on days gone by.

MODERN RAILWAYS

Aimed, as its name suggests, at the enthusiast of the railway scene today, it provides news on all the goings-on and analysis of performance and operation.

7

MODEL RAILWAYS

Perhaps you hanker after the nostalgia of the railways of old, wishing you could recreate the excitement of *Mallard*'s 126mph record run, or the glory of some of the magnificent long-lost railway termini or the rural idyll of a country branch line. Maybe there's a railway near you that's long since closed and you wish you could see trains running on it once more, or possibly you've always wanted to be a driver or a signalman. While none of this might be possible in real life, it can all be achieved in model form.

﷽ HOW THE HOBBY ﷽ DEVELOPED

With trains holding a fascination for many from their earliest days, it wasn't long before the first basic models began to appear. Most were primitive and toy-like, bearing only a passing resemblance to the real thing. Today, though, model railways are quite sophisticated, far removed from the train sets of even 20 or 30 years ago. The earliest ones, made in the Victorian era, were made of tinplate and white metal and had locomotives powered by clockwork. They were much larger than what we tend to think of as model railways today. Electricity began to be used to power models around the turn of the 20th century, but even then the motors were large, making the trains cumbersome and crude.

As technology moved on, the trains and track got smaller and more detail was added, and it's now possible to build an authentic miniature recreation of the real thing no matter how little space you have.

‖‖‖ SCALE AND GAUGE ‖‖‖

Two terms you'll hear bandied about a lot in the world of model railways are 'scale' and 'gauge'. At first glance, these may seem interchangeable – you hear 'OO' scale and 'OO' gauge used to describe the same models – but they aren't and it's important to understand the difference. The **scale** of a model refers to its size as a proportion of the real thing, and in Britain you'll hear it described as a peculiar mix of millimetres and feet. The **gauge** refers to the distance between the rails.

From the smallest to the largest of the most popular scales and gauges the list is as follows:

- **'Z' scale:** 1.385mm: 1 foot or 1:220; track gauge = 6.5mm

- **'N' scale:** 2mm: 1 foot or 1:144 (1:160 in Europe); track gauge = 9mm

- **'HO' scale:** 3.5mm: 1 foot or 1:87 (used for Continental models); track gauge = 16.5mm

- **'OO' scale:** 4mm: 1 foot or 1:76 (used for British models); track gauge = 16.5mm

- **'O' scale:** 7mm: 1 foot or 1:43.5; track gauge = 32mm

'Z' SCALE

Very little 'Z' scale equipment is available in Britain, principally because there are virtually no models of British rolling stock available in this smallest of scales.

'N' SCALE

'N' scale is more popular, with a reasonable amount of British outline rolling stock available and stocked at many model shops. Nonetheless, there are still a vast number of common locomotives and coaches that are not supplied in ready-to-run model form in this scale. Modellers of American and Continental practice are well-catered for, however.

'HO' SCALE

'HO' scale is mostly used in mainland Europe, as very few British models have ever been made. 'HO' locomotives, wagons and coaches can all run on the track systems used by the more common 'OO' scale, making it easy for those modelling in this scale to develop their model railways.

'OO' SCALE

'OO' scale is the most popular in Britain, with a vast range of locomotives, rolling stock, scenery, buildings and other lineside structures available as off-the-shelf items in model shops all across the country. The standard of models in this scale has increased significantly in recent years, and many locomotives look as good straight out of the box as of the hand-built ones made by skilled modellers.

'O' SCALE

'O' scale was most popular before the Second World War, with many of the tinplate trains of the day being made in this scale. In recent times 'O' scale modelling has improved in standard and fine scale ready-made track is available. A handful of ready-made models are available but these are very expensive. Most locomotives and other rolling stock comes in kit form, making this scale more suited to experienced modellers.

Pocket Fact 🚂

The early tinplate models, though crude, were well-made and many survive in working order, although not all are in good condition and mint boxed examples are highly sought-after collector's items today. If you like the nostalgia of the 1930s and aren't concerned with mint condition items, you can relive the glory days with your own tinplate model railway!

⧼⧽ PLANNING A MODEL ⧼⧽ RAILWAY

With the old 'O' scale trains it was the norm to simply set the track out on the living room carpet and start running trains; the track and rolling stock were designed with this in mind, with robust construction taking priority over scale appearance. This is no longer the case with modern models, and setting up a new train set on the carpet is probably one of the worst things you can do. Carpet fluff can ruin locomotive mechanisms and track can be bent and damaged easily. For that reason, the track is best fixed to a baseboard made from plywood or chipboard and framed with softwood on its underside to ensure it is flat; when the track is fixed to the board it's referred to as a layout.

For this reason, the most important consideration for a model railway is deciding where it will go and working out the space you have available to build it. Don't underestimate the space a layout can take up. A basic 'OO' scale oval of track will need a baseboard of around 6ft × 4ft (1.8m × 1.2m) in size when allowance is made for a few buildings and some scenery. Taking into account things like stations and sidings, a space of 8ft × 6ft (2.4m × 1.8m) is ideal.

Many modern houses now have quite small rooms and so it can be difficult to find a home for a layout of these proportions. This is the main reason many people choose a smaller scale; an 'N' scale layout, using track half the size, will fit in a space a quarter of the size (that is, half the length and half the width) of a comparable 'OO' scale one. So the 8ft × 6ft 'OO' layout referred to above will require only 4ft × 3ft (1.2m × 0.9m) in 'N'; small enough to fit beneath a single bed. Of course, if you have the space for the larger-sized layout, you can have effectively four times the track length on the same baseboard.

POSSIBLE AREAS FOR LAYOUTS

- A spare room is the ideal location for a model railway, as temperature and humidity are usually fairly constant.

- A garage, attic or loft space is also suitable, as long as it's insulated and isn't subject to extremes of temperature as these can play havoc with both the timber of the baseboard and the electrical joints on the track and wiring.

- The lounge or dining room is also a feasible location, as a layout can be run on a narrow shelf around the room (allowing a little more space around the corners) without encroaching too much on the room itself. If you're inventive enough, it's possible to make covers to protect the layout when it's not in use and disguise it to fit in with existing furniture.

- In a similar way it's possible to build a layout round the edge of a bedroom that would otherwise not have space for a layout. The important thing to consider in these situations is access into the room, so a lifting or removable section of baseboard will be required across the doorway if a continuous run of track is required.

BEYOND THE HOUSE

If you can't find anywhere indoors for a layout of the size you want, you may be able to find a space outside. A timber garden shed can be made into a suitable layout room by insulating it and adding power, heat and light. Something as simple as an electric convector heater can keep the space from getting too cold and damp as long as there are no leaks. It's also possible to build a layout in the garden itself, though the larger scales ('O' scale and above) are usually better suited to this.

Pocket Fact

One of the largest and most famous outdoor model railways is situated at Bekonscot Model Village in Beaconsfield, Buckinghamshire. It is Gauge 1 (45mm gauge, 10mm:1 foot scale) and is 450 metres in length (around 10 scale miles). To find out more, and get a 'driver's eye view' of this extensive model railway, visit www.bekonscot.co.uk.

⊞⊞⊞ TRAIN SETS ⊞⊞⊞

Assuming you've identified a suitable available space for a layout, the way that most people begin in the hobby is with a train set. These usually come with a locomotive, a few carriages or wagons, a circle or oval of track and a controller (often mistakenly called a transformer, it converts the mains electricity supply to a variable low-voltage supply to control the trains).

The variety of sets is daunting, ranging from inexpensive, basic ones containing a small shunting locomotive and three wagons, to top-of-the-range sets with an express passenger locomotive and coaches. The basic ones tend to be aimed at children, with brightly coloured and less detailed (and therefore less delicate) rolling stock, priced from about £60 upwards. There are also a number of 'character' sets, including Thomas the Tank Engine and Underground Ernie. The more expensive sets (costing from around £100) are aimed at adult modellers, with better quality models and controllers and finer detailing.

Thomas the Tank Engine

Thomas the Tank Engine first appeared in 1946, in the second book in the Reverend Wilbert Awdry's famous 'Railway Series'. There were 26 books in the original series, published between 1945 and 1972. Awdry based most of his stories on actual occurrences and always in accordance with the rules of the railway; the only departure from reality was that the locomotives had faces and talked, but they still required a driver and fireman in order to work.

Further stories have been produced in recent times, though other than using some of the original characters they differ significantly from Awdry's original works and the rights are now owned by HiT Entertainment. Nonetheless, Thomas and his friends are still popular throughout the world.

Train sets can be bought on the internet, possibly at a slight discount on the full retail price, but the sheer variety of them means that selecting the most suitable one from a picture on a website can be difficult. For that reason, it's best to go to a specialist model shop to look at the sets first hand, and get advice from the knowledge of the proprietors. You may also find some sets (or the shop may be able to make you a set up) that are second-hand, giving you considerably more for your money.

⧚⧚⧚ CHOICE OF CONTROL ⧚⧚⧚

Traditionally, trains on a model railway are controlled by a device (a controller) that varies the voltage to the rails, typically between 0V and 14V, to vary the speed of the train. The direction of the train is changed by changing the polarity of the rails, usually by flicking a switch on the controller. You will need a controller for each separate track, so if you have a double track loop you will need two controllers (or a double controller with two separate outputs).

This method of control is very simple, but it does have certain disadvantages; for example if you have more than one locomotive on the same track, each one will move at the same time when the power is applied from the controller. The way to prevent this is to isolate pieces of track you wish to hold stationary trains on by having an insulating break in the rails, linking the sections with a piece of wire via a switch. With just a few isolating sections, this method is quite acceptable, but on larger layouts it can become quite cumbersome.

DIGITAL COMMAND CONTROL

In recent years, computer technology has entered the world of model railways and a method of control known as DCC (Digital Command Control) is becoming more common. Using this method, the track is constantly supplied with electric current and each locomotive is fitted with a decoder chip. The controller can send commands to each chip, telling it to start or stop a train, and setting the speed and direction. Once a train is moving, it will continue to move until told to stop by the controller, and it is possible to control several trains at once on the same track with just one controller (or handset). DCC allows locomotives to be fitted with sound decoders and speakers, so realistic train noise actually comes from the locomotive! It also allows trains to be fitted with lighting that stays on all the time, and some DMU models (such as Bachmann's Class 108) come with working head and tail lamps and full interior lighting.

The setup of DCC can be more complicated and more expensive for a basic circuit; the controllers themselves are significantly more costly than conventional ones (which these days are described as analogue controllers) and the locomot ives all have to be fitted with chips, costing from £10 each. There are a number of DCC starter sets available, so ask in a specialist model shop for advice on what's the best setup for you.

Pocket Tip

A number of specialist shops advertise in some of the railway modelling magazines, notably Railway Modeller, Hornby Magazine, British Railway Modelling *and* Model Rail. *There's bound to be one near to you so check it out.*

BUILDING BASEBOARDS

For your model railway to be reliable in operation, a good sturdy base on which to affix the track is essential. There are many complicated ways to make baseboards, but if you're just starting with a set the simplest ways are usually adequate. For a robust board, use a sheet of 9mm or 12mm (3/8 inch or 1/2 inch) plywood braced at 600mm (24 inch) intervals with 50mm × 25mm (2 inch × 1 inch) softwood. When choosing the bracing, choose long, straight pieces with as few knots as possible. To keep cost down and get the best quality materials, try going to your nearest timber merchant rather than a DIY superstore. The timber merchant will usually be able to cut your boards and soft-wood to the correct size, either for free or for a nominal sum.

When assembling the baseboard, for longevity it's best to use PVA glue and screws to attach the bracing to the top; avoid using nails if possible as they have a tendency to work loose if the board flexes.

⊞⊞⊞ LAYING THE TRACK ⊞⊞⊞

There are two types of track available in both 'N' and 'OO' scales, namely set track (as supplied in train sets but also sold separately; set track comes in fixed length straight and fixed radius curved sections) and flexible track (also called 'streamline' track). Flexible track can be bent into almost any curved shape andtrains tend to run more smoothly along it than they do on set track. However, it is extremely tricky to lay as it has to be carefully cut to length after bending. For this reason, it's best avoided until you've gained some experience of railway modelling.

First, you need to decide on a suitable trackplan to work to. The basic oval that comes with a train set will become operationally boring very quickly, and at the very least a number of sidings can be added to provide further interest. There are a number of track-plan books available, including the Setrack Planbooks for 'OO' and 'N' scale, produced by the company Peco, which also manu-factures good quality track in both scales. Hornby also produce 'OO' scale track and plans. If you choose a trackplan from one of these books, next to it you will find a list of all the different track sections you'll require to replicate the plan on your layout. Once you've built the baseboard and purchased the track, you're ready to make a start.

The track sections are joined by metal joiners called fishplates, which are very delicate, requiring the track to be exactly in line when it's pushed together to prevent them being damaged. The track can be laid directly on the baseboard, on foam underlay or on a layer of cork. The latter two methods help to cut down noise,

TURNOUTS (POINTS)

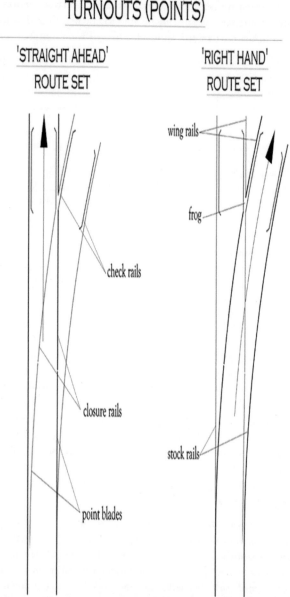

'STRAIGHT AHEAD' ROUTE SET

check rails

closure rails

point blades

'RIGHT HAND' ROUTE SET

wing rails

frog

stock rails

as the grinding sound of the motors can otherwise be magnified through the baseboard. The track can be pinned down using special track pins, which are available from model shops. There are holes already present in the sleepers of most sectional track, allowing the pins to be inserted and pushed home lightly with a tack hammer. When positioning the track, allow a small gap between each rail section to allow the rails to expand when the temperature increases.

POINTS

Just like the real thing, points (more correctly referred to as turnouts) are used to allow trains to move between different tracks on a model railway. A wide variety are available: both left- and right-handed, to suit different radii on curved track, and also insulated (to isolate tracks) and non-insulated (which are much harder to work with as they require some complex wiring). Again, pointwork is quite a complicated subject and it would be beneficial to seek advice from a specialist model shop or choose the turnouts specified in your book of trackplans. The location of the points will also affect the position of the clip that feeds power to the track from the controller; again, this will be clearly identified on the trackplan.

Pocket Tip

Dirt can build up very quickly on rail surfaces, particularly with track fed from an analogue controller. This is because the rails gain a slight electrostatic charge from the electricity supply, which attracts dirt particles. The dirt then sticks to the top of the rails, preventing the electric current from flowing through the locomotive's wheels to the motor and making the train jerk to a halt whenever a dirty section of track is encountered. To prevent this, use a track rubber to gently scrub the dirt away, but don't press too hard on delicate pointwork as it can easily become damaged.

SCENERY

With the track laid, it's time to start thinking about buildings and scenery. A good place to start is with a station platform and buildings. Many ready-made structures are available, together with kits from plastic and cardboard. The ready-made items include platform sections and buildings, which can simply be placed straight on the layout; while this is the quickest solution it is by no means inexpensive.

The quality of the plastic building kits available is excellent, and with a little time and patience it is possible to produce as good a result as using a ready-made building at around half the cost. The cardboard kits are by far the cheapest, and as they come ready-printed and punched out, they just require a little glue and patience to complete.

With buildings and platforms placed but not fixed, select your longest coach and push it around the track, checking it does not catch on anything. With that accomplished, it's time to think about the landscape through which the trains will run. The world isn't flat, and your layout will look more realistic if you add some small hills or undulations around the track. This can be done very easily, using a variety of materials readily available from model shops. For small hillocks and such, the simplest method is to use strips of plaster bandage laid over scrunched-up newspaper, while for bigger hills, cutting slopes and the like, the plaster bandage can be laid over wire mesh (such as chicken wire) fastened to contoured wooden formers.

GROUND COVER

With the basic shape of the landscape established, the surface can be applied. For roadways, dark grey paint sprinkled with talcum powder while it's still wet is inexpensive and convincing. For grassed areas, flock and scenic scatter materials are available from model shops. Flock consists of short fibres in a variety of colours, while scenic scatter is a cheaper option consisting of dyed sawdust. First, apply green or brown paint as a basic ground cover, and apply the flock or scatter onto the wet paint. Scenic scatter can be applied by hand, while flock is best applied from a puffer bottle which encourages the fibres to stand on end, simulating long grass quite realistically.

Trees

A number of proprietary trees are available, either ready-made or as kits. Recently some very realistic ready-made models of actual tree species are being produced, though the cost of these is quite high and the size of even the largest is somewhat under scale for 'OO' scale models. Cheaper ready-made trees are also available; these have a trunk of twisted wire and polyester bristles for branches, and resemble coloured bottle brushes. Nonetheless, the effect can be quite good if they are used in a group to represent a small copse.

Many other items, including fences, street furniture, scale vehicles, people and animals are also available, and all will help to make the layout look realistic and bring it to life.

⊞⊞⊞ ROLLING STOCK ⊞⊞⊞

The locomotive and handful of wagons or coaches that came with your train set will no doubt spark your interest, but before long you're bound to want to add variety to your collection. These days, you're sure to be able to find the locomotives, wagons and coaches you need as ready-to-run items on the shelf at your local model shop; literally hundreds of different ones are now made.

You can, of course, buy second-hand items to reduce outlay, but many of the older models don't run as smoothly as more up-to-date ones and it's always best to seek advice at your nearest specialist shop. From the 1970s until the early 2000s, some manufacturers made steam locomotives with the motors in the tenders rather than in the locomotive itself, and the running qualities of some of these leave a lot to be desired. Recently improvements in quality and detail have been made across the board by all manufacturers, and new locomotives will pull longer trains and run more smoothly and quietly than those made in the last century.

The story is the same for coaches and wagons; new models now all have turned metal wheels, which run more smoothly and produce less dirt on the rails than the moulded plastic ones previously used. The axles usually run in proper bearings, decreasing friction (which means longer trains can be pulled by the same locomotive) and reducing the risk of derailments. Their chassis are now carefully weighted, again helping them to stay on the track and run more smoothly. While buying second-hand coaches and wagons can save you a considerable amount of money, it's better if you can inspect them before buying – it's essential that the wheels turn freely without binding or 'wobble' (the latter caused by badly-moulded plastic axles).

MANUFACTURERS OF NEW ROLLING STOCK

'OO' scale rolling stock

Hornby

The name everyone thinks of first for model railways, Hornby have recently updated many of their models to have a higher level of detail and better running qualities. This comes at a cost and makes the models more fragile. Recognising that the younger modellers need something a little more robust and less expensive, Hornby have also recently introduced their Railroad range, often using older tooling but still with good quality mechanisms. This makes them an ideal starting point for expanding a collection. Hornby also produce ready-made buildings and other accessories.

Bachmann

Bachmann's models are of superb quality, and have offered a good level of detail combined with relatively sturdy mechanisms for a good many years. A wide variety of steam and diesel locomotives are manufactured, and they also make the Junior range aimed at younger modellers (though this is not as extensive as Hornby's Railroad range). They also make various wagons and coaches to the same high standard, and some ready-made buildings and accessories are offered to accompany the range.

Heljan

Heljan manufacture a small number of British outline models of diesel and electric locomotives. They have recently made models of some of the more unusual classes and one-off prototypes as well. Running qualities are generally good and the level of detail is also good. They also make a number of modern-image wagons to accompany the locomotives.

ViTrains

ViTrains produce models of the Class 37 and Class 47 diesel locomotives at the time of writing, though they plan to expand their range.

Dapol

Dapol originally made locomotives, wagons and coaches in 'OO' scale, but the bulk of the range was sold to Hornby in recent years and Dapol now concentrate on manufacturing wagons only. These are of a high quality with plenty of detail and they run well.

'N' scale rolling stock

Graham Farish by Bachmann

Graham Farish has always been the principal manufacturer of British outline 'N' scale. Originally British-owned with all products made in Dorset, the business was sold to Bachmann in 2001 and production moved to China. There was a shortage of products for many years until production gathered pace, but now Bachmann have improved the quality and range of the rolling stock significantly, with new models launched each year.

Dapol

A relatively recent addition to the 'N' scale market, Dapol make a small number of locomotives, coaches and wagons including a

'9F' 2-10-0 and a diminutive Great Western '14XX' 0-4-2T Auto Tank and matching coach.

Peco
Renowned for making good quality track for many years, Peco also make 'N' scale wagons (both as easy-to-assemble kits and ready-to-run) and have recently introduced a Great Western Railway Collett '2251' class 0-6-0 goods locomotive to their range.

⊞⊞⊞ EXHIBITIONS AND CLUBS ⊞⊞⊞

If you like the idea of a model railway but aren't quite sure how to begin, why not go along to a model railway exhibition and have a look at some of the layouts there? These are popular events that run from autumn to spring, and there's sure to be one near to you. There will often be specialist trade stands, and the staff and exhibitors are usually only too pleased to share advice with visitors. If you see a feature you like on a layout that you'd like to replicate on your own, don't be afraid to ask how it was created. A list of exhibitions and dates can be found in most of the model railway publications mentioned earlier.

The best way to develop your modelling skills is undoubtedly to join a model railway club. Members usually meet at a dedicated club house once a week or more, and work on either a club lay-out or one or more belonging to members. There are usually modellers of various scales there, and you'll be able to develop your skills faster under their guidance. To find your nearest model railway club, you can either ask at an exhibition, do an internet search or ask at your local model shop where the staff are likely to have details as the club members often call in for supplies.

Pocket Tip

A good place to find second-hand bargains is a swapmeet or a toy or train fair. These events are held up and down the country, and are effectively an indoor market where the only things on offer are railway models, and there's usually a small entry charge. Price and condition of items can vary significantly but the events are very popular — get there early to bag a bargain! In particular, they are a great place to find rare collector's items including tinplate trains. A list of swapmeets and fairs is published monthly in Railway Modeller magazine.

GLOSSARY

Automatic Train Control (ATC)
Pioneered by the Great Western Railway from 1906, this was an electrically operated safety device which could sound a warning hooter in the cab of a locomotive if a distant signal (see pp26–27) was approached at caution. It could also apply the brakes, though this action could be cancelled by the driver.

Automatic Warning System (AWS)
A development of the Great Western Railway's Automatic Train Control (see above), this system was introduced by British Railways and worked on all types of signal. Again, if a signal was passed at caution or danger it could apply the brakes, but this action could be over-ridden by the driver.

Blastpipe
The pipe through which exhaust steam passes into the smokebox from the cylinders. The steam shoots through the chimney and expands into the atmosphere, causing a partial vacuum in the smokebox which is used to draw air through the fire and help it to draw.

Bogie coach
A coach fitted with a pivoting 4- or 6-wheeled truck (or 'bogie') under each end, which provides smooth and stable travel for its passengers.

Boiler
The long barrel above the frames on a steam locomotive, in which the steam is made. The fire is contained in the firebox at the cab end, and the exhaust steam, soot and ashes are sent out via the chimney on the smokebox at the front end.

Brake van
A heavy van used at the end of a freight train. These contained a handbrake and accommodation for the guard, and usually had a

viewing platform at one or both ends to enable the guard to keep an eye on the train.

Catenary
A system of overhead wires, supported on gantries or cantilevers from the lineside, that supplies the electric traction current for some types of trains.

Connecting rod
The rod that connects the piston in the cylinder to the driving wheels of a locomotive.

Continuous brake
A brake that can be applied from the locomotive which acts on all vehicles in a train at once. Two systems are used: vacuum brakes, which sucks air out of a pipe to pull the brakes off and, if air leaks in, the brakes are applied; and air brakes, which work the opposite way, using compressed air.

Corridor tender
A tender behind a steam locomotive, through which a narrow corridor runs that allows locomotive crews to move from the train to the footplate while the train is in motion.

Coupling
The device that connects together the vehicles in the train.

Coupling rods
The rods used to join the driving wheels together on each side of a locomotive.

Cutting
An open channel excavated through an obstacle (such as a steep hill or mountain) through which a railway line runs.

Diesel Multiple Unit
A train formed of self-powered coaches (called cars) with a driving cab contained at each end. The train is powered by diesel engines and a number of the units can be coupled together to make longer trains.

Diesel railcar

Similar to a Diesel Multiple Unit, a diesel railcar is one or more self-powered coaches with a driving cab at either end and powered by diesel engines. Unlike a diesel multiple unit, a railcar cannot work in multiple with other units.

Disc and Crossbar signal

An early form of signal designed by Brunel. It had a flat disc and a rectangular bar fastened to a pole at right angles (see the diagram on p.27). When the crossbar was displayed to the train the signal was at danger, but when the pole rotated through 90 degrees, the disc was displayed indicating 'line clear'.

Electric Multiple Unit

A train formed of self-powered coaches (called cars) with a driving cab contained at each end. The train is powered by electric motors and a number of the units can be coupled together to make longer trains.

Embankment

A man-made bank of earth upon which a railway runs, used to carry the line across dips in the landscape.

Flange

A protruding lip on the inside of a rail-mounted wheel, which sits on the inside of the rail and keeps the train on the track, effectively steering it.

Footplate

The name given to a steam locomotive's cab where the driver and fireman sit or stand to control the train.

Fourth rail

A system of carrying electric current to supply trains. In addition to the two running rails that carry the train's wheels, there are two other rails; one carries the traction current (positive current) and is situated on the ends of the sleepers outside the rails, and the other supplies the return current (negative current) and is located in the centre of the two running rails. It is used extensively on the London Underground.

Gauge
The distance between the rails on which a train's wheels run.

Mercury arc rectifier
A means of converting alternating current from the supply to direct current suitable for the traction motors. They are very efficient but use liquid mercury in their operation, which is a potential hazard in a locomotive.

OTMR
Stands for 'On Train Monitoring and Recording', this equipment is fitted to most locomotives and trains that run on the national network. It's effectively the railway equivalent of the black box fitted to aircraft.

Pannier tank
A locomotive that has water tanks fastened to either side of the boiler. The tanks do not meet at the top, nor do they reach the chassis at the bottom of the boiler and their name thus comes from the similar panniers carried by pack horses.

Points (turnouts)
A device used to move trains from one track to another. See the diagram on p.158 for an explanation.

Railmotor
A steam-powered version of a railcar, it is a railway coach that has a boiler and steam engine located at one end, driving a small powered bogie. They were never very successful in Britain, but one is being restored to working order at Didcot Railway Centre.

Saddle tank
A locomotive that carries a single water tank that sits across the top of the boiler and hangs down on either side, similar to the way a saddle sits on a horse.

Semaphore signal
The name given to a mechanical device that has a horizontal arm that moves either up or down to give a 'danger', 'caution' or 'line clear' signal. They are also fitted with coloured lenses that show a red, yellow or green light at night or in fog.

Side tank
A locomotive with a pair of water tanks that extend upwards from the chassis on either side of the boiler.

Sleeping car
A coach containing a number of compartments which each contain one or more beds (known as berths). Used extensively on overnight trains all over the world, with some still in operation in Britain.

Smoke deflectors
Shaped screens fitted either side of the smokebox to encourage smoke to lift.

Smokebox
The section at the front of the boiler where the soot, ash and air from the fire are mixed with the exhaust steam from the cylinders of a steam locomotive.

Third rail
A system of carrying electric current to supply trains. In addition to the two running rails that carry the train's wheels, there is an extra rail to carry the traction current (positive current) which is situated on the ends of the sleepers outside the rails. The return current (negative current) is carried by the running rails. The system is used extensively in the south-east of England.

TOPS (Total Operations Processing System)
The system introduced by British Rail to number its locomotives and multiple units; still in use today. Classes are described by their prefix number, for example a Class 37 diesel might be numbered 37 676 and a Class 390 Pendolino might be 390 004.

TPWS
Stands for 'Train Protection and Warning System'. A development of the previous Automatic Warning System, it automatically applies the brakes if a train passes a signal at danger or if it exceeds a speed limit on the line. Unlike earlier systems, its action can't be overruled by the driver; the incident has to be telephoned through to a control centre for the system to be reset remotely.

Unfitted train

A train of wagons that is not fitted with the continuous brake. Instead, the train will have a brake van at the rear and handbrakes on the wagons that must be individually applied before descending a steep hill.

Valve Gear

A series of rods that change the gearing of a steam locomotive.

Well tank

A locomotive that has a water tank fixed between the frames of its chassis beneath the cab or boiler.

THE DAD'S
POCKET BIBLE

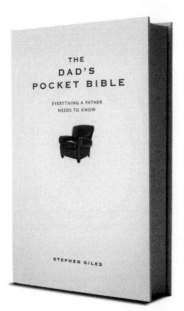

The Dad's Pocket Bible is the perfect gift for a number one dad. Brimming with artful tips, handy hints and brilliant pointers for fathers; from rainy day fun with the kids to finding that all important shed time, say thanks to your dad with this perfect pocket companion.

978-1-90708-702-8

Available now

£9.99

www.pocketbibles.co.uk

THE GOLF
POCKET BIBLE

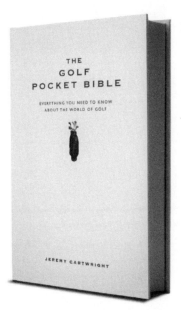

Whether you're a golfing pro or simply a Sunday driver, immerse yourself in *The Golf Pocket Bible* and discover the fascinating world of golf. From the game's history and modern day popularity, to the fairways, famous tournaments and golfing legends.

978-1-90708-711-0

Available now

£9.99

POCKET
BIBLES
www.pocketbibles.co.uk

THE FOOTBALL
POCKET BIBLE

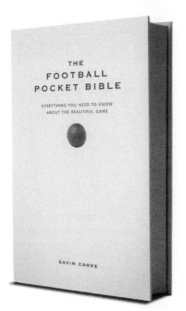

Every fan knows that football is much more than just a game: it's the beautiful game. Immerse yourself in the world's favourite sport with *The Football Pocket Bible*, from its rich history and modern day rules to the beloved clubs, prestigious trophies and footballing heroes.

978-1-90708-710-3

Available now

£9.99

www.pocketbibles.co.uk